Ordnance Survey

Cycle Tours

24 one-day routes in

North Wales
and the
Marches

Compiled by
Nick Cotton

PHILIP'S

Contents

On-road routes

4 Key to routes

6 Quick reference chart

8 North Wales and the Marches

9 Abbreviations and instructions

10 Fact boxes
Page diagrams

11 Before you go

12 Cross-profile diagrams

13 Tips for touring

15 Transporting your bike

16 Legend to 1:50 000 maps

18 1 Rolling lanes across Anglesey

24 2 In and out of the Conwy Valley

30 3 Through the Clwyd Hills, north from Denbigh

36 4 Hills, forests and reservoirs, southwest of Denbigh

42 5 Lakes and passes in the Berwyn Mountains

48 6 Along the Ceiriog Valley, west of Oswestry

54 7 Through the Cheshire Plain around Whitchurch

60 8 Into the hills above the Dovey Valley from Machynlleth

66 9 Hills and reservoirs, east of Aberystwyth

72 10 Towards the source of the River Severn, west of Llanidloes

78 11 Bishop's Castle, Montgomery and the Kerry Ridgeway

84 12 The Long Mynd, from Church Stretton

90 13 Steep Welsh Border countryside north of Knighton

96 14 Tributaries of the River Teme, west of Ludlow

Off-road routes

102 1 Into hills above the coast to the west of Conwy

106 2 Mountain tracks and a Roman road near Betws-y-Coed

110 3 Two waymarked routes in Gwydir Forest Park, Betws-y-Coed

114 4 The heart of the Clwyd Hills, west from Nannerch

118 5 East from Ruthin into the southern Clwyd Hills

122 6 Into the Berwyn Mountains, west of Oswestry

126 7 Along the Mawddach Estuary, west of Dolgellau

130 8 The Dovey Estuary and Happy Valley, west of Machynlleth

134 9 Vyrnwy Valley and Dyfnant Forest north of Llangadfan

138 10 The Wye Valley and Hafren Forest, west of Llangurig

Back cover photograph: the view south from Llanddwyn Island towards the LLeyn Peninsula

First published 1997 by

Ordnance Survey and George Philip Ltd, an imprint of
Romsey Road   Reed Books
Maybush   Michelin House
Southampton   81 Fulham Road
SO16 4GU   London SW3 6RB

Text and compilation
Copyright © Reed International Books Ltd 1997
Maps Copyright © Crown Copyright 1997

The route maps in this book are based upon Ordnance Survey® Landranger® mapping.

The cross-profile diagrams in this book have been created using Ordnance Survey® Land-Form PANORAMA™ Digital height data.

Ordnance Survey and Landranger are registered trade marks and Land-Form PANORAMA is a trade mark of Ordnance Survey, the National Mapping Agency of Great Britain.

First edition 1997

A catalogue record for this atlas is available from the British Library

ISBN 0 600 59007 0
Printed in Spain

Acknowledgements
AA Photo Library 37, 49 • Nick Cotton 123 • Derek Forss 31, 97, 115, 119 • Colin Molyneux back cover, 19, 43, 46, 55, 61, 67, 73, 85, 88, 92, 127, 131, 135 • David Tarn 107, 112 • Judy Todd 25, 91, 103 • edited by Melissa Arnison-Newgass • designed by Ian Muggeridge • picture research by Jenny Faithfull • production by Claudette Morris • art editor: James Hughes

Key to routes

Legend

8 (diamond)	On-road cycle route
8 (diamond)	Off-road cycle route
M4 (S)	Motorway, service area
18 — 19	Junction, limited access
A31	Primary route
A684	Other main road
Dover	City / major town
○ Mere	Primary town
○ Yate	Other town

Primary routes form a national network of recommended through routes which complement the motorway system

The primary towns shown on this map appear on traffic signs which, on primary routes, have a green background or, on motorways, have a blue background

	County boundary
	National boundary
- - - - -	Domestic ferry route
	Passenger railway
✈ ✈(circle)	Airport / with customs
(H)	Heliport
	National parks, forest parks and areas of scenic beauty

```
0        10        20        30 km
0            10            20 miles
```

Scale 1:1 000 000 1 cm to 10 km or about 1 inch to 16 miles

IRISH SEA

Amlwch
A5025
Holyhead ISLE OF ANGLESEY
ANGLESEY
A5
A4080
Menai Bridge
Bangor
A55
Conwy
Llandudno
Rhyl
FLIN
Colwyn Bay
Abe
A548
Den
CONWY
Llanrwst
A543
Betws-y-Coed
A5
Llyn Brenig
A4086
A4085
Caernarfon
A487
A498
GWYNEDD
Caernarfon Bay
Nefyn
A499
Porthmadog
Ffestiniog
A4212
Snowdonia
Bala
A497
Pwllheli
Harlech
A470
A494
Lleyn
A499
Abersoch
A496
Dolgellau
Barmouth
A493
Tywyn
A489
Machynlleth
CARDIGAN BAY
A487
A470
CAMBRIAN MOUNTAINS
Aberystwyth
A44
A4120
Aberaeron
A485
CEREDIGION
New Quay
Tregaron
A482
Afon Teifi
A487
Cardigan
A486
A475
Lampeter
A482
Llanwrtyd Wells
A483
A470
Newcastle Emlyn
A484
A485
Llandovery
St David's Head
A487
Fishguard
A40
Pembrokeshire Coast
A478
CARMARTHENSHIRE
A483
St David's
PEMBROKESHIRE
Llandeilo
A40
A4069
Brecon
Haverfordwest
Narberth
St Clears
Carmarthen
Afon Tywi
Rhayader
Llanwrtyd Wells

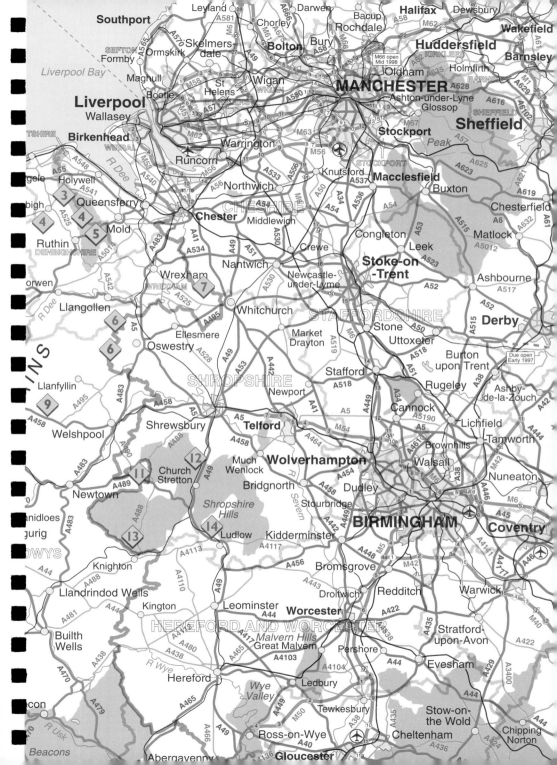

Quick reference chart

Route		Page	Distance (kilometres)	Grade (easy/moderate/strenuous)	Links with other routes[1]	Tourist information centres[2]
On-road routes						
1	Rolling lanes across Anglesey	18	57	◖◖		Llanfair PG 01248 713177
2	In and out of the Conwy Valley	24	67	◖◖◖◖◖		Conwy 01492 592248
3	Through the Clwyd Hills, north from Denbigh	30	53	◖◖◖◖◖	4	Mold 01352 759331
4	Hills, forests and reservoirs, southwest of Denbigh	36	55	◖◖◖◖◖	3	Ruthin 01824 703992
5	Lakes and passes in the Berwyn Mountains	42	54	◖◖◖◖◖		Bala * 01678 521021
6	Along the Ceiriog Valley, west of Oswestry	48	47	◖◖◖◖		Oswestry 01691 662883
7	Through the Cheshire Plain around Whitchurch	54	47	◖		Whitchurch 01948 664577
8	Into the hills above the Dovey Valley from Machynlleth	60	61	◖◖◖◖◖	10	Machynlleth 01654 702401
9	Hills and reservoirs, east of Aberystwyth	66	59	◖◖◖◖◖		Aberystwyth 01970 612125
10	Towards the source of the River Severn, west of Llanidloes	72	43	◖◖◖	8	Llanidloes 01686 412605
11	Bishop's Castle, Montgomery and the Kerry Ridgeway	78	61	◖◖◖◖◖		Knighton 01547 528753
12	The Long Mynd, from Church Stretton	84	37	◖◖◖		Church Stretton 01694 723133
13	Steep Welsh Border countryside north of Knighton	90	51	◖◖◖◖◖	14	Knighton 01547 528753
14	Tributaries of the River Teme, west of Ludlow	96	47	◖◖◖	13	Ludlow 01584 875053

Route	Page	Distance (kilometres)	Grade (easy/moderate/strenuous)	Links with other routes [1]	Tourist information centres [2]
Off-road routes					
1 Into hills above the coast to the west of Conwy	102	29	/////		Conwy 01492 592248
2 Mountain tracks and a Roman road near Betws-y-Coed	106	23	////	3	Betws-y-Coed 01690 710246
3 Two waymarked routes in Gwydir Forest Park, Betws-y-Coed	110	18½ 12½	///	2	Betws-y-Coed 01690 710246
4 The heart of the Clwyd Hills, west from Nannerch	114	29/20	///// ///	5	Mold 01352 759331
5 East from Ruthin into the southern Clwyd Hills	118	30	/////	4	Ruthin 01824 703992
6 Into the Berwyn Mountains, west of Oswestry	122	20	/////		Oswestry 01691 662883
7 Along the Mawddach Estuary, west of Dolgellau	126	43 24½	///// /// /		Dolgellau 01341 422888
8 The Dovey Estuary and Happy Valley, west of Machynlleth	130	25	/////		Machynlleth 01654 702401
9 Vyrnwy Valley and Dyfnant Forest north of Llangadfan	134	34	/////		Welshpool 01938 552043
10 The Wye Valley and Hafren Forest, west of Llangurig	138	35	/////		Llanidloes 01686 412605

[1] **Links with other routes** Use this information to create a more strenuous ride or if you are planning to do more than one ride in a day or on a weekend or over a few days. The rides do not necessarily join: there may be a distance of about 5 km (3 miles) between the closest points. Several rides are in pairs, sharing the same starting point, which may be a good place to base yourself for a weekend.

[2] **Tourist Information Centres** You can contact them for details about accommodation. If they cannot help, there are many books that recommend places to stay. If nothing is listed for the place where you want to stay, try phoning the post office or the pub in the village to see if they can suggest somewhere. * Open from Easter to the end of September only.

North Wales and the Marches

North Wales summons up images of big hills, particularly Snowdonia which is one of Britain's most mountainous areas. Indeed hills, moorland and forest-clad upland very much dominate the region covered by this book. Often the best routes through the valleys are taken up by the busy main roads and so the quiet lanes that climb up over the hills inevitably make a series of challenging bike routes linking market towns with outlying villages and remote farmsteads.

For those seeking easier cycling there are a few, limited opportunities: the island of Anglesey is undulating rather than hilly and is criss-crossed with small lanes; the Lon Eifion railway path runs south from the wonderful castle in Caernarfon to the small village of Bryncir; another delightful railway path runs along the Mawddach Estuary; to the east there is a flat circuit around Lake Vyrnwy; there are quiet, gentle lanes in the Vale of Clwyd and finally, the pastureland near Whitchurch in the area between Shrewsbury and Chester. Other options are to follow the easier of the waymarked trails in the Forestry Commission holdings, particularly those at Coed y Brenin.

It would be misleading, however, to suggest that there is much easy cycling in North Wales and the Marches: this is tough cycling country with fabulous rewards for those fit enough to contemplate the hills. It is one of the least populated regions in Great Britain and there are huge areas with little but sheep, trees, buzzards, red kites and the odd, outlying farmhouse. On-road routes start from the attractive castle towns of Conwy and Denbigh, from the coast at Aberystwyth and in the heart of the Principality from Llanidloes, Machynlleth and Bala. Five routes are based in the border county of Shropshire with starting points ranging from the lovely old, half-timbered town of Ludlow in the south to the bustling market town of Oswestry in the north.

The off-road cycling picture is mixed: there are few bridleways in the most northern part of Wales and those in Snowdonia are also very popular with walkers. There is a voluntary agreement in place which asks bikers not to use the bridleways to the summit of Snowdon between 10 am and 5 pm from 1st June until 30th September. This has been very successful and created a lot of goodwill; please stick to it for the sake of our continued access to other similar areas. A better mountain biking area is the Clwyd Range, west of Chester.

Abbreviations and instructions

*I*nstructions are given as concisely as possible to make them easy to follow while you are cycling. Remember to read one or two instructions ahead so that you do not miss a turning. This is most likely to occur when you have to turn off a road on which you have been riding for a fairly long distance and these junctions are marked **Easy to miss** to warn you.

If there appears to be a contradiction between the instructions and what you actually see, always refer to the map. There are many reasons why over the course of a few years instructions will need updating as new roads are built and priorities and signposts change.

If giving instructions for road routes is at times difficult, doing so for off-road routes can often be almost impossible, particularly when the route passes through woodland. With few signposts and buildings by which to orientate yourself, more attention is paid to other features, such as gradient and surface. Most of these routes have been explored between late spring and early autumn and the countryside changes its appearance very dramatically in winter. If in doubt, consult

your map and check your compass to see that you are heading in the right direction.

Where I have encountered mud I have mentioned it, but this may change, not only from summer to winter but also from dry to wet weather, at any time during the year. At times you may have to retrace your steps and find a road alternative.

Some routes have small sections that follow footpaths. The instructions will highlight these sections where you must get off and push your bike. You may only ride on bridleways and by-ways so be careful if you stray from the given routes.

Directions

L	left
LH	left-hand
RH	right-hand
SA	straight ahead or straight across
bear L or R	make less than a 90-degree (right-angle) turn at a fork in the road or track or at a sharp bend so that your course appears to be straight ahead; this is often written as *in effect SA*
sharp L or R turn	is more acute than 90 degrees
sharp R/L back on yourself	an almost U-turn
sharp LH/RH bend	a 90-degree bend
R then L or R	the second turning is visible then immediately L from the first
R then 1st L	the second turning may be some distance from the first; the distance may also be indicated: *R, then after 1 mile L*

Junctions

T-j	T-junction, a junction where you have to give way
X-roads	crossroads, a junction where you may or may not have to give way
offset X-roads	the four roads are not in the form of a perfect cross and you will have to turn left then right, or vice versa, to continue the route

Signs

'Placename 2'	words in quotation marks are those that appear on signposts; the numbers indicate distance in miles unless stated otherwise
NS	not signposted
trig point	a trigonometrical station

Instructions

An example of an easy instruction is:

4 At the T-j at the end of Smith Road by the White Swan PH R on Brown Street 'Greentown 2, Redville 3'.

There is more information in this instruction than you would normally need, but things do change: pubs may close down and signs may be replaced, removed or vandalized.

An example of a difficult instruction is:

8 Shortly after the brow of the hill, soon after passing a telephone box on the right next L (NS).

As you can see, there is no T-junction to halt you in your tracks, no signpost indicating where the left turn will take you, so you need to have your wits about you in order not to miss the turning.

Fact boxes

The introduction to each route includes a fact box giving useful information:

Start

This is the suggested start point coinciding with instruction 1 on the map. There is no reason why you should not start at another point if you prefer.

Distance and grade

The distance is, of course, that from the beginning to the end of the route. If you wish to shorten the ride, however, the maps enable you to do so.

The number of drinks bottles indicates the grade:

Easy

Moderate

Strenuous

Page diagrams

The on-road routes usually occupy four pages of mapping each. The page diagrams on the introductory pages show how the map pages have been laid out, how they overlap and if any inset maps have been used.

This section of the route is shown on pages 92 and 93

This overlap area appears at the foot of pages 92 and 93 and at the top of pages 94 and 95

This area is shown as an inset on page 94

This section of the route is shown on pages 94 and 95

92   93
94   95

The grade is based on the amount of climbing involved.

Remember that conditions may vary dramatically with the weather and seasons, especially along off-road sections

Terrain

This brief description of the terrain may be read in conjunction with the cross-profile diagram at the foot of the page to help you to plan your journey.

Nearest railway

This is the distance to the nearest station from the closest point on the route, not necessarily from the start. Before starting out you should check with British Rail for local restrictions regarding the carrying of bicycles.
(See page 15)

Refreshments

Pubs and teashops on or near the route are listed. The tankard symbols indicate pubs particularly liked by the author.

Before you go

Fitness

❁ Cycling uses muscles in a different way from walking or running, so if you are beginning or returning to it after a long absence you will need time to train your muscles and become accustomed to sitting on a saddle for a few hours. Build up your fitness and stamina gradually and make sure you are using a bicycle that is the right size for you and suits your needs.

Equipment

❁ Attach the following items to the bike: bell, pump, light-brackets and lights, lock-holder and lock, rack and panniers or elastic straps for securing things to the rack, map holder. Unless it is the middle of summer and the weather is guaranteed to be fine, you will need to carry extra clothes, particularly a waterproof, with you, and it is well worth investing in a rack for this purpose.

❁ Wearing a small pouch around your waist is the easiest and safest way of carrying small tools and personal equipment. The basics are: Allen keys to fit the various Allen bolts on your bike, chainlink extractor, puncture repair kit, reversible screwdriver (slot and crosshead), small adjustable spanner, spare inner tube, tyre levers (not always necessary with mountain bike tyres), coins and a phonecard for food and telephone calls, compass.

❁ Additional tools for extended touring: bottom bracket extractor, cone spanners, freewheel extractor, headset spanners, lubricant, socket spanner for pedals, spare cables, spoke-key.

Clothing

❁ What you wear when you are cycling should be comfortable, allowing you, and most especially your legs, to move freely. It should also be practical, so that it will keep you warm and dry if and when the weather changes.

❁ **Feet** You can cycle in just about any sort of footwear, but bear in mind that the chain has oil on it, so do not use your very best shoes. Leather tennis shoes or something similar, with a smooth sole to slip into the pedal and toe clip are probably adequate until you buy specialist cycling shoes, which have stiffer soles and are sometimes designed for use with specialist pedals.

❁ **Legs** Cycling shorts or padded cycling underwear worn under everyday clothing make long rides much more comfortable. Avoid tight, non-stretch trousers, which are very uncomfortable for cycling and will sap your energy, as they restrict the movement of your legs; baggy tracksuit

11

bottoms, which can get caught in the chain and will sag around your ankles if they get wet. Almost anything else will do, though a pair of stretch leggings is probably best.

Upper body What you wear should be long enough to cover your lower back when you are leaning forward and, ideally, should have zips or buttons that you can adjust to regulate your temperature. Several thin layers are better than one thick layer.

Head A helmet may protect your head in a fall.

Wet weather A waterproof, windproof top is essential if it looks like rain. A dustbin bag would be better than nothing but obviously a breathable waterproof material is best.

Cold weather A hat that covers your ears, a scarf around your neck, a pair of warm gloves and a thermal top and bottom combined with what you would normally wear cycling should cover almost all conditions.

Night and poor light Wearing light-coloured clothes or reflective strips is almost as important as having lights on your bike. Reflective bands worn around the ankles are particularly effective in making you visible to motorists.

Preparing your bicycle

You may not be a bicycle maintenance expert, but you should make sure that your bike is roadworthy before you begin a ride.

If you are planning to ride in soft, off-road conditions, fit fat, knobbly tyres. If you are using the bike around town or on a road route, fit narrower, smoother tyres.

Check the tyres for punctures or damage and repair or replace if necessary or if you are in any doubt. Keep tyres inflated hard (recommended pressures are on the side wall of the tyre) for mainly on-road riding. You do not need to inflate tyres as hard for off-road use; slightly softer tyres give some cushioning and get better traction in muddy conditions.

Ensure that the brakes work efficiently. Replace worn cables and brake blocks.

The bike should glide along silently. Tighten and adjust any part that is loose or rubbing against a moving part. Using a good-quality bike oil lubricate the hubs, bottom bracket, pedals where they join the cranks, chain and gear-changing mechanism from both sides. If the bike still makes grating noises, replace the bearings.

Adjust the saddle properly. The saddle height should ensure that your legs are working efficiently: too low and your knees will ache; too high and your hips will be rocking in order for your feet to reach the pedals. Some women find the average bike saddle uncomfortable because the female pelvis is a different shape from the male pelvis and needs a broader saddle for support. Some manufacturers make saddles especially for women.

Cross-profiles

The introduction to each route includes a cross-profile diagram. The blue grid indicates 1-kilometre horizontal intervals and 50-metre vertical intervals

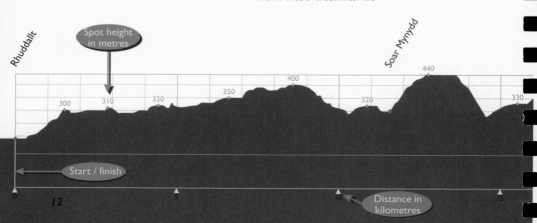

Tips for touring

The law

In England and Wales there are 193 000 km (120 000 miles) of rights of way but under the Wildlife and Countryside Act of 1968 you are allowed to cycle on only about 10 percent of them, namely on bridle-ways, by-ways open to all traffic (BOATS) and roads used as public paths (RUPPS).

The other 90 percent of rights of way are footpaths, where you may walk and usually push your bike, but not ride it. Local bylaws sometimes prohibit the pushing of bicycles along footpaths and although all the paths in this book have been checked, bylaws do sometimes change.

⚙ You are not allowed to ride where there is no right of way. If you lose the route and find yourself in conflict with a landowner, stay calm and courteous, make a note of exactly where you are and then contact the Rights of Way Department of the local authority. It has copies of definitive maps and will take up the matter on your behalf if you are in the right.

Cycling techniques

If you are not used to cycling more than a few kilometres at a stretch, you may find initially that touring is tiring. There are ways of conserving your energy, however:

⚙ Do not struggle in a difficult gear if you have an easier one. Let the gears help you up the hills. No matter how many gears a bike has, however, ultimately it is leg power that you need to get you up a hill. You may decide to get off and walk uphill with your bike to rest your muscles.

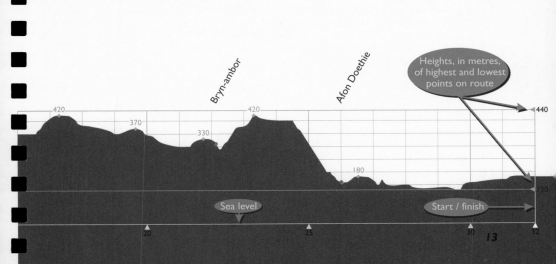

You can save a lot of energy on the road by following close behind a stronger rider in his or her slipstream, but do not try this offroad. All the routes are circular, so you can start at any point and follow the instructions until you return to it. This is useful when there is a strong wind, as you can alter the route to go into the wind at the start of the ride, when you are fresh, and have the wind behind you on the return, when you are more tired.

The main difference in technique between on-road and off-road cycling lies in getting your weight balanced correctly. When going down steep off-road sections, lower the saddle, keep the pedals level, stand up out of the saddle to let your legs absorb the bumps and keep your weight over the rear wheel. Control is paramount: keep your eyes on what lies ahead.

Traffic

The rides in this book are designed to minimize time spent on busy roads, but you will inevitably encounter some traffic. The most effective way to avoid an accident with a motor vehicle is to be highly aware of what is going on around you and to ensure that other road users are aware of you.

Ride confidently.

Indicate clearly to other road users what you intend to do, particularly when turning right. Look behind you, wait for a gap in the traffic, indicate, then turn. If you have to turn right off a busy road or on a difficult bend, pull in and wait for a gap in the traffic or go past the turning to a point where you have a clear view of the traffic in both directions, then cross and return to the turning.

Use your lights and wear reflective clothing at night and in poor light.

Do not ride two-abreast if there is a vehicle behind you. Let it pass. If it cannot easily overtake you because the road is narrow, look for a passing place or a gate entrance and pull in to let it pass.

Maintenance

Mountain bikes are generally stronger than road bikes, but any bike can suffer. To prevent damage as far as possible:

Watch out for holes and obstacles.

Clean off mud and lubricate moving parts regularly.

Replace worn parts, particularly brake blocks.

Riders also need maintenance:

Eat before you get hungry, drink before you get thirsty. Dried fruit, nuts and chocolate take up little space and provide lots of energy.

Carry a water bottle and keep it filled, especially on hot days. Tea, water and well-diluted soft drinks are the best thirst-quenchers.

Breakdowns

The most likely breakdown to occur is a puncture.

Always carry a pump.

Take a spare inner tube so that you can leave the puncture repair until later.

Make sure you know how to remove a wheel. This may require an adjustable spanner or, in many cases, no tool at all, as many bikes now have wheels with quick-release skewers that can be loosened by hand.

Security

Where you park your bike, what you lock it with and to are important in protecting it from being stolen.

Buy the best lock you can afford.

Lock your bike to something immovable in a well-lit public place.

Locking two bikes together is better than locking them individually.

Use a chain with a lock to secure the wheels and saddle to the frame. Keep a note of the frame number and other details, and insure, photograph and code the bike.

Transporting your bike

*T*here are three ways of getting you and your bike to the start of a ride:

Cycle to the start or to a point along a route near your home.

Take the train. Always check in advance that you can take the bike on the train. Some trains allow only up to two bikes and you may need to make a reservation and pay a flat fee however long the journey. Always label your bike showing your name and destination station.

Travel by motor vehicle. You can carry the bikes:

- Inside the vehicle. With the advent of quick release mechanisms on both wheels and the seatpost, which allow a quick dismantling of the bike, it is possible to fit a bike in even quite small cars. It is unwise to stack one bike on top of another unless you have a thick blanket separating them to prevent scratching or worse damage. If you are standing them up in a van, make sure they are secured so they cannot slide around.

- On top of the vehicle. The advantages of this method are that the bikes are completely out of the way and are not resting against each other, you can get at the boot or hatch easily and the bikes do not obscure the number plate or rear lights and indicators. The disadvantages are that you use up more fuel, the car can feel uncomfortable in a crosswind and you have to be reasonably tall and strong to get the bikes on and off the roof.

- On a rack that attaches to the rear of the vehicle. The advantages are that the rack is easily and quickly assembled and disassembled, fuel consumption is better and anyone can lift the bikes on and off. The disadvantages are that you will need to invest in a separate board carrying the number plate and rear lights if they are obstructed by the bikes, you cannot easily get to the boot or hatch once the bikes have been loaded and secured, and the bikes are resting against each other so you must take care that they don't scrape off paint or damage delicate parts.

- Whichever way you carry the bikes on the outside of the vehicle, ensure that you regularly check that they are secure and that straps and fixings that hold them in place have not come loose. If you are leaving the bikes for any length of time, be sure they are secure against theft; if nothing else lock them to each other.

Legend to 1:50 000 maps

Roads and paths

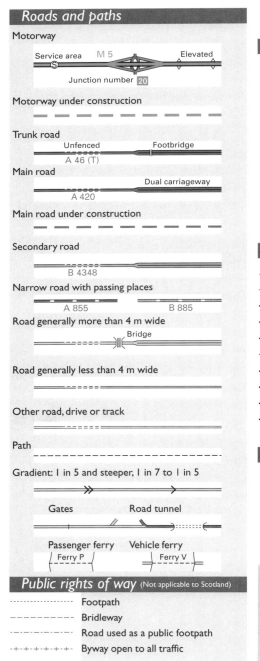

Motorway

Service area   M 5   Elevated

Junction number 20

Motorway under construction

Trunk road
Unfenced   Footbridge
A 46 (T)

Main road
Dual carriageway
A 420

Main road under construction

Secondary road
B 4348

Narrow road with passing places
A 855   B 885

Road generally more than 4 m wide
Bridge

Road generally less than 4 m wide

Other road, drive or track

Path

Gradient: 1 in 5 and steeper, 1 in 7 to 1 in 5

Gates   Road tunnel

Passenger ferry   Vehicle ferry
Ferry P   Ferry V

Public rights of way (Not applicable to Scotland)

········· Footpath
– – – – – Bridleway
–·–·–·– Road used as a public footpath
–+–+–+– Byway open to all traffic

Danger Area   Firing and test ranges in the area.
Danger! Observe warning notices

Tourist information

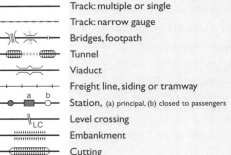

ℹ ℹ	Information centre, all year / seasonal
P	Parking
✕	Picnic site
☀	Viewpoint
Å	Camp site
🚐	Caravan site
▲	Youth hostel
	Selected places of tourist interest
☏	Public telephone
☏	Motoring organisation telephone
⌐	Golf course or link
PC	Public convenience (in rural areas)

Railways

Track: multiple or single
Track: narrow gauge
Bridges, footpath
Tunnel
Viaduct
Freight line, siding or tramway
Station, (a) principal, (b) closed to passengers
Level crossing   LC
Embankment
Cutting

Rock features

outcrop   cliff   650   600   scree

Public rights of way indicated by these symbols have been derived from Definitive Maps as amended by the latest enactments or instruments held by Ordnance Survey and are shown subject to the limitations imposed by the scale of mapping. Further information may be obtained from the appropriate County or London Borough Council

The representation on this map of any other road, track or path is no evidence of the existence of a right of way

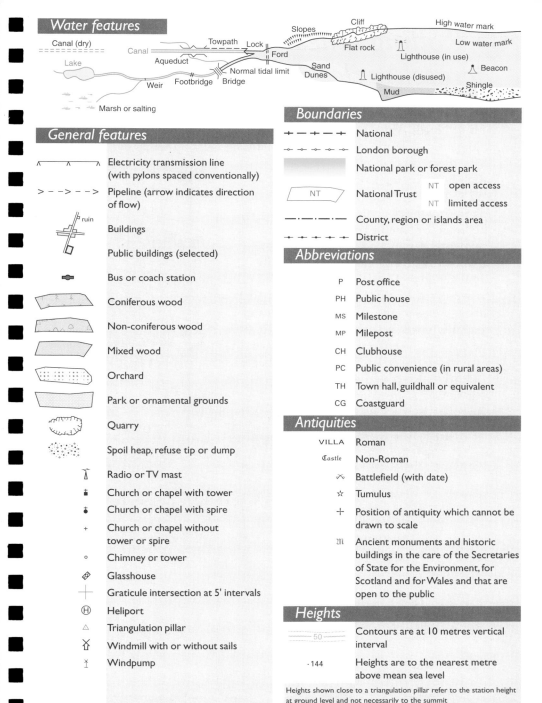

Water features

Canal (dry)
Canal
Lake
Towpath
Aqueduct
Weir
Footbridge
Bridge
Lock
Ford
Normal tidal limit
Marsh or salting
Slopes
Cliff
Flat rock
Sand Dunes
Mud
High water mark
Low water mark
Lighthouse (in use)
Lighthouse (disused)
Beacon
Shingle

General features

∧——∧——∧	Electricity transmission line (with pylons spaced conventionally)
> - -> - ->	Pipeline (arrow indicates direction of flow)
ruin	Buildings
	Public buildings (selected)
	Bus or coach station
	Coniferous wood
	Non-coniferous wood
	Mixed wood
	Orchard
	Park or ornamental grounds
	Quarry
	Spoil heap, refuse tip or dump
	Radio or TV mast
	Church or chapel with tower
	Church or chapel with spire
+	Church or chapel without tower or spire
○	Chimney or tower
	Glasshouse
	Graticule intersection at 5' intervals
Ⓗ	Heliport
△	Triangulation pillar
	Windmill with or without sails
	Windpump

Boundaries

+ — + — +	National
—○—○—○—○—	London borough
	National park or forest park
NT	National Trust
	NT open access
	NT limited access
—·—·—·—	County, region or islands area
+ + + +	District

Abbreviations

P	Post office
PH	Public house
MS	Milestone
MP	Milepost
CH	Clubhouse
PC	Public convenience (in rural areas)
TH	Town hall, guildhall or equivalent
CG	Coastguard

Antiquities

VILLA	Roman
Castle	Non-Roman
✕	Battlefield (with date)
☆	Tumulus
+	Position of antiquity which cannot be drawn to scale
ℳ	Ancient monuments and historic buildings in the care of the Secretaries of State for the Environment, for Scotland and for Wales and that are open to the public

Heights

‑‑50‑‑	Contours are at 10 metres vertical interval
·144	Heights are to the nearest metre above mean sea level

Heights shown close to a triangulation pillar refer to the station height at ground level and not necessarily to the summit

17

Rolling lanes across Anglesey

Anglesey presents a total contrast to the rest of North Wales and offers many kilometres of gentle cycling on quiet lanes. With the exception of half a dozen small hills Anglesey does not rise above 152 m (500 ft). The ride starts from Llanfairpwllgwyngyll, the village with the longest name in Britain, as you will be frequently reminded by some very long signposts. The village itself is normally abbreviated to Llanfair PG. The island is criss-crossed by tiny lanes which meander through arable and pasture land heading generally northwest then southwest to join the coast at Aberffraw. As the ride turns away from the coast and heads northeast back to the start you will enjoy some of the best views of Snowdonia in the whole region.

Refreshments

Plenty of choice in
Llanfairpwllgwyngyll
Prince Llewelyn PH, Y Goron PH,
tea rooms, **Aberffraw**
Royal Oak PH, Joiners Arms PH,
Malltraeth

Start

Railway station,
Llanfairpwllgwyngyll,
5 km (3 miles) west of
Bangor

P At the railway
station

Distance and grade

57 km (35 miles)

Easy/moderate

Terrain

Gently rolling agricultural land and sand dunes near Aberffraw. Total height gain –
455 m (1495 ft)

Nearest railway

Llanfairpwllgwyngyll

Llanfairpwllgwyngyll

Llanfair PG | Afon Braint | Afon Ceint | Talwrn | Langwyllog | Llynfaes | Gwalchmai Uchaf

65 48 75 64 62

0   5   10   15   20   25

Aberffraw 13

The village was the capital of North Wales from AD 870 until the 13th century. The Norman-style arch in the church of St Bueno is said to have come from the destroyed palace of the Llywelyns. A packhorse bridge crosses the River Ffraw

St Cwyfan's Church 3 km (2 miles) off the route near 13

A small church built 1300 years ago and restored in 1893. It has a spectacular setting on a rock between two coves, Porth Cwyfan and Porth China. It is reached by causeway at low tide

Llanddwyn Bay and Newborough Warren
5 km (3 miles) off the route near 17

A vast wilderness of sand, marram-grass dunes and Forestry Commission plantations. At the western end is Llanddwyn Island, a nature reserve where shags and cormorants breed, connected to the mainland by a narrow neck of land

▼ Menai Strait and Snowdonia, from Anglesey

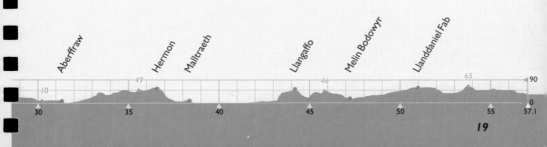

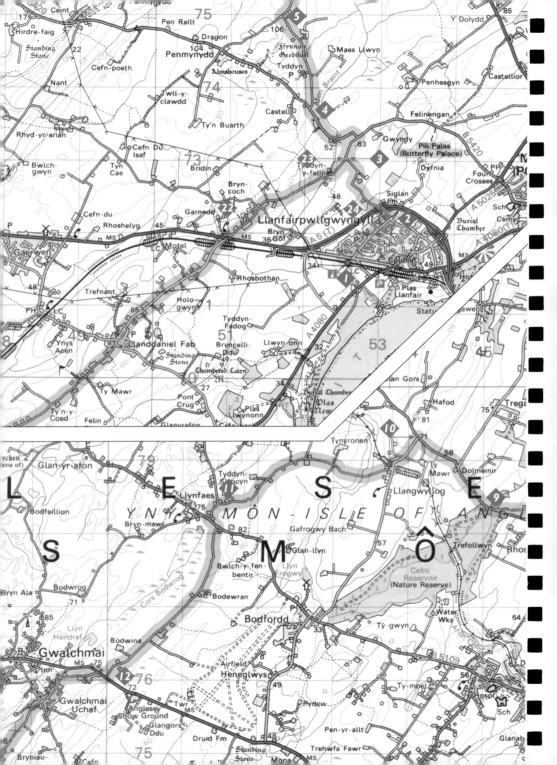

1 Exit Llanfair PG Railway Station, turn R then 1st L opposite Ty Gwyn Post Office

2 After 1 km, on a sharp RH bend, turn L onto Fford Penmynydd

3 At T-j R (NS) then shortly, at next T-j (with B5420), L (NS)

4 After 1 km 1st R 'Eglwys Church'

5 At T-j next to church R 'Rhoscefnhir, A5025'

6 At T-j L 'Talwrn, Llangefni'

7 Descend to cross dismantled railway. Climb. At T-j by Give Way sign R

8 Ignore right and left turns for 4 km (2½ miles). At T-j (with B5110) L 'Llangefni A5', then shortly R (NS)

9 At T-j with busy road (B5111) R

10 After 1 km 1st L 'Llangwyllog, Bodffordd (A5)' then **easy to miss**, after 800 m (½ mile), immediately after crossing railway bridge next R

11 At T-j with red tiled bungalow ahead L. At T-j with B5109 L 'Bodffordd, Llangefni', then R

12 At T-j (with A5) R, then L

➡ page 23

22 Continue SA, ignoring right and left turns for 8 km (5 miles) (and leaving Bike Route 8). At X-roads with A5 SA

23 Climb, descend, cross stream and start climbing, then next R 'Llanfair PG'

24 At T-j at the end of Fford Penmynydd, R. At T-j at the bottom of the hill R to return to the start

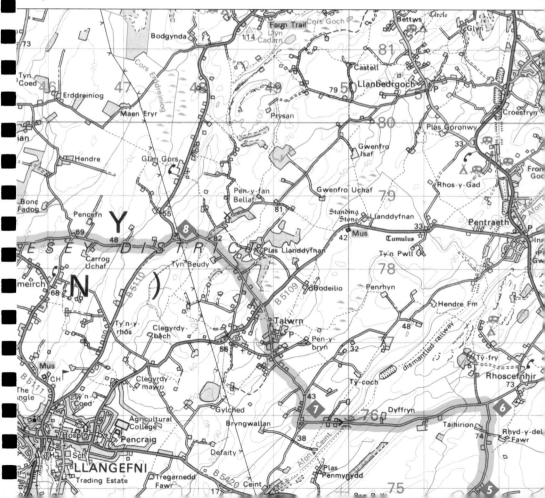

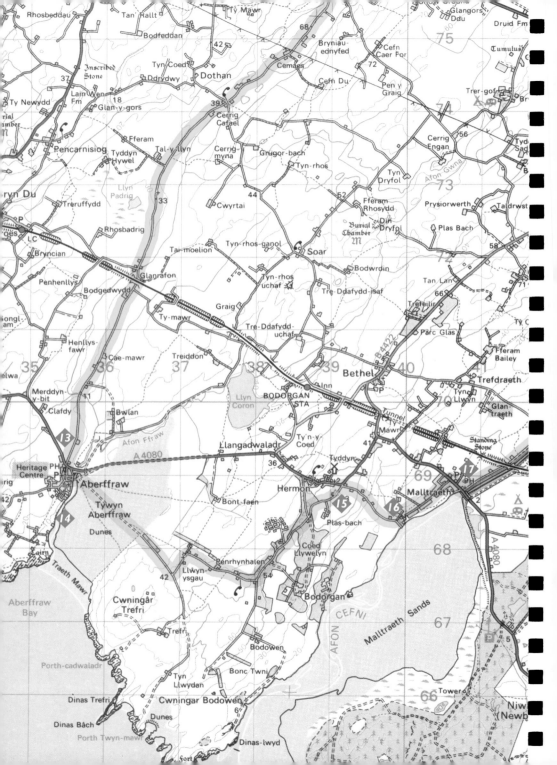

13 *Follow for 10 km (6 miles). At T-j with A4080 L 'Newborough', then R 'Village Centre'*

14 *At Y Goron PH L downhill to cross the bridge and bear R*

15 *After 5 km (3½ miles) at junction with A4080 on sharp bend turn R down 'No through road'*

16 *After 800 m (½ mile), towards the bottom of the hill turn L onto concrete track then, just before LH bend, bear R along footpath for 180 m (200 yd) (dismount and push bike along footpath). At tarmac lane L*

17 *At T-j with A4080 R, then 1st L after Joiners Arms 'Glan-traeth Animal Park'*

18 *After 3 km (2 miles) 1st R over bridge 'Bike Route 8'*

19 *At offset X-roads with B4419 R, then L 'Dwyran, Brynsiencyn'*

20 *Descend, then climb. Near the brow of hill 1st L 'Bike Route 8'*

21 *At T-j after the burial chamber in the field to the left turn L 'Bike Route 8'*

◀ page 21

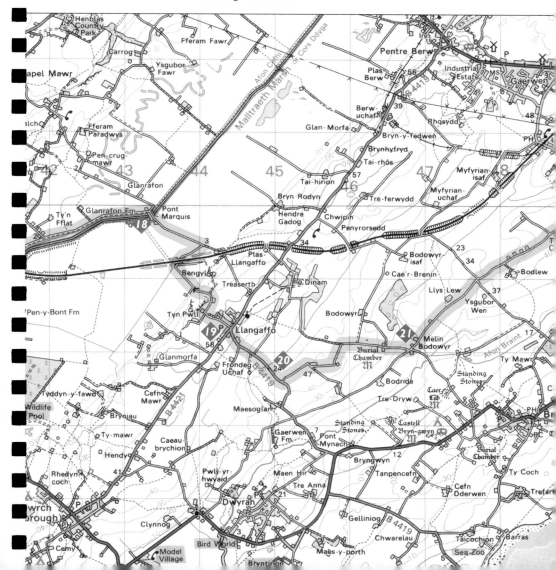

In and out of the Conwy Valley

For a ride which ostensibly follows the course of the River Conwy from its estuary at the sea, south to Betws-y-Coed, there is an awful lot of climbing with six hills of over 90 m (300 ft), one of 213 m (700 ft) and numerous smaller climbs. This is the toughest on-road route in the book and makes a full day's outing but it could be shortened by crossing the valley at Llanrwst. The route follows quiet lanes through picturesque farmland beneath the high fells to the west, parallel to the valley trunk road. The B5106 is unavoidably joined for about 7 km (4 miles) south to Trefriw before the longest and steepest climb of the day past Llyn Geirionydd and down through Gwydir Forest into Betws-y-Coed. You soon escape onto the network of quiet lanes that cross the River Conwy heading north to the second high point of the ride. A descent through woodland leads to Llanrwst and past the small lake of Llyn Syberi before re-crossing the river, rejoining the outward route and returning to Conwy.

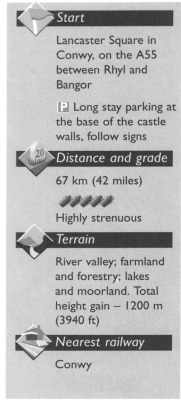

Start

Lancaster Square in Conwy, on the A55 between Rhyl and Bangor

P Long stay parking at the base of the castle walls, follow signs

Distance and grade

67 km (42 miles)

Highly strenuous

Terrain

River valley; farmland and forestry; lakes and moorland. Total height gain – 1200 m (3940 ft)

Nearest railway

Conwy

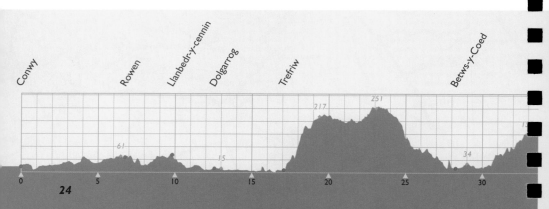

▲ *Conwy Castle*

Places of interest

Conwy 1

One of the best-preserved, medieval, fortified towns in Britain with battlemented walls, narrow gateways and Edward I's great castle (built 1283-92). There are three bridges over the River Conwy – Telford's 1826 suspension bridge, Robert Stephenson's tubular railway bridge of 1848 and a modern road bridge. There are over 200 listed buildings, some dating back as far as 1300. Don't miss a walk along the old town walls in Conwy

Llanrwst 21

An elegant, 17th-century, three-arched bridge, attributed to Inigo Jones, spans the River Conwy in this old market town. Gwydir Castle is a Romantic Tudor mansion, built in 1555 and restored in the 1940s. Cedars of Lebanon, growing in the landscaped gardens, were planted to mark the wedding of Charles I in 1625

Refreshments

Plenty of choice in **Conwy**
Ty Gwyn Hotel, **Rowen**
Olde Bull Inn 🍴🍷, **Llanbedr-y-cennin**
Y Bedol PH. **Tal-y-Bont**
Lord Newborough PH, **Dolgarrog**
Trfriw Wells Spa tea shop, between **Dolgarrog** and **Trefriw**
Ye Olde Shippe Inn, Fairy Falls Hotel, **Trefriw**
Plenty of choice in **Betws-y-Coed**
Plenty of choice in **Llanwrst**
Tal-y-cafn Inn 🍷, **Tal-y-cafn**

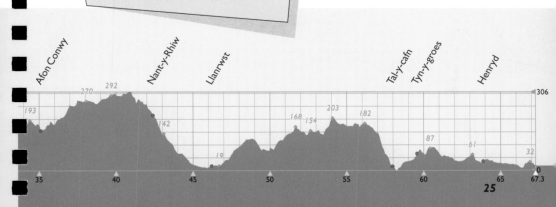

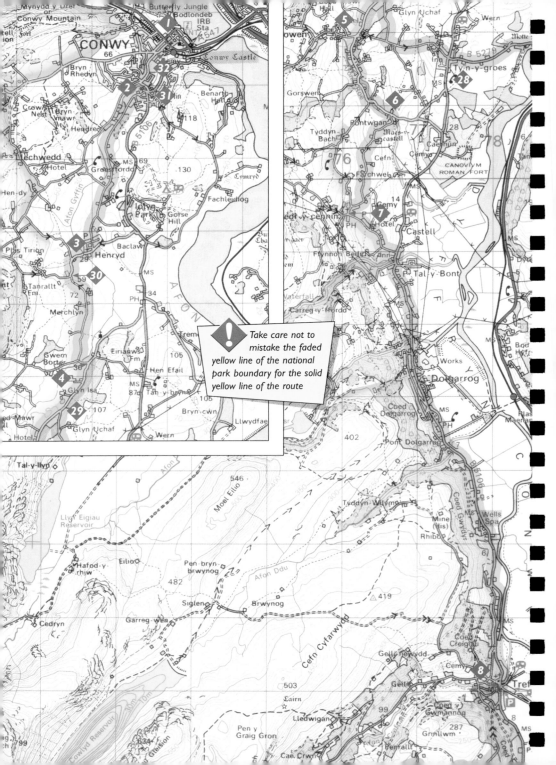

Take care not to mistake the faded yellow line of the national park boundary for the solid yellow line of the route

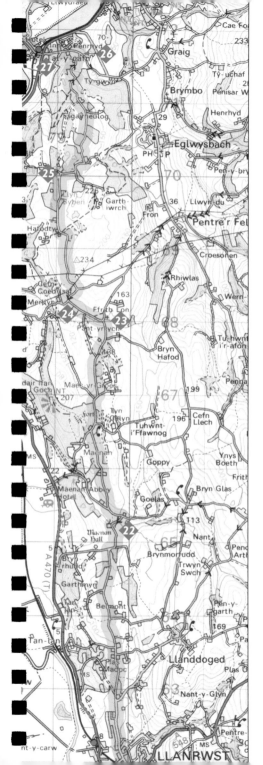

1 From Lancaster Square in Conwy head uphill towards town walls. 1st L by Albion PH onto Upper Gate Street. Exit town walls, then 1st L onto St Agnes Road

2 At T-j with B5106 R onto Henryd Road 'Henryd 1½'

3 After 3 km (2 miles), at T-j R (NS), then after 800 m (½ mile), shortly after the start of the climb 1st L steeply uphill 'Rowen'

4 After 1 km at T-j R 'Trout – Coarse fishing. Pysgota'

5 Just after the Rowen Post Office and before 'Rowen' village sign turn L to continue along the valley

6 **Ignore** 1st R after 1 km opposite stone bridge over the river. Take the next R by a small triangle of grass and a letter box to re-cross the river

7 At T-j in Llanbedr-y-cennin by Olde Bull Inn L downhill. At T-j with B5106 R 'Trefriw' (this road is fairly busy)

8 After 8 km (5 miles), in Trefriw – shortly after woollen mills, Fairy Falls Hotel and bridge over the river, next R. At T-j after short steep climb L (NS)

➡ **page 29**

22 Ignore several right and left turns over 5 km (3 miles). At T-j by triangle of grass and bench L 'Eglwysbach 2½'

23 **Easy to miss**. Ignore several left and right turns and drives to farmhouses over next 3 km (2 miles). At the bottom of a sharp dip with a small slate-roofed barn to the right turn L gently uphill

24 At T-j R steeply uphill towards pylons. Follow road round to the L and beneath two sets of power lines

25 At the end of small lake follow road sharply R uphill

26 At T-j at the end of Fford Llyn Syberi L, then **easy to miss** on steep descent 1st R

27 At offset X-roads with A470 at Tal-y-cafn Hotel L, then R and cross bridge

28 Climb. At X-roads with B5106 by the Red Lion PH SA. Climb, descend, climb again. 1st R (NS)

29 At T-j by small triangle of grass turn R to rejoin outward route. Ignore left to Glyn Isa Fishery. Take next L 'Henryd'

30 At T-j at the bottom of short, steep hill R 'Henryd', then turn L by the school in Henryd

31 At T-j with the B5106 by Post Office L

32 At T-j at the end of St Agnes Road R. Through the town walls. At T-j by the Albion PH dismount and turn R to return to Lancaster Square

27

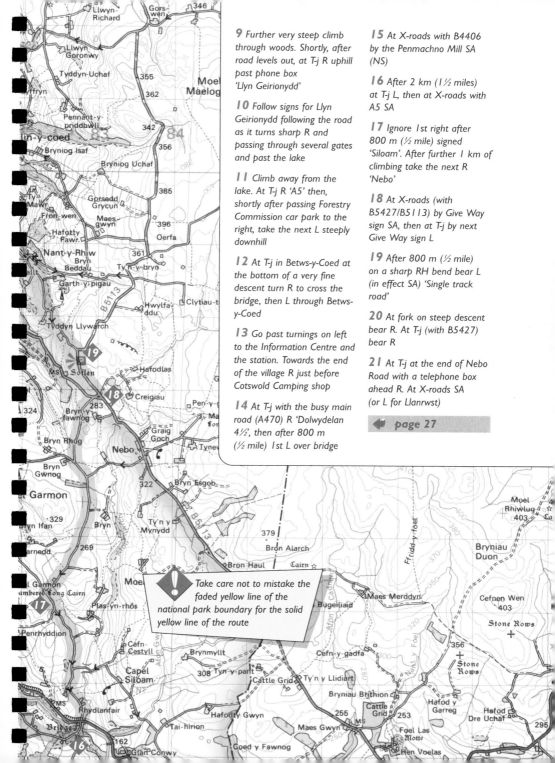

9 Further very steep climb through woods. Shortly, after road levels out, at T-j R uphill past phone box 'Llyn Geirionydd'

10 Follow signs for Llyn Geirionydd following the road as it turns sharp R and passing through several gates and past the lake

11 Climb away from the lake. At T-j R 'A5' then, shortly after passing Forestry Commission car park to the right, take the next L steeply downhill

12 At T-j in Betws-y-Coed at the bottom of a very fine descent turn R to cross the bridge, then L through Betws-y-Coed

13 Go past turnings on left to the Information Centre and the station. Towards the end of the village R just before Cotswold Camping shop

14 At T-j with the busy main road (A470) R 'Dolwydelan 4½', then after 800 m (½ mile) 1st L over bridge

15 At X-roads with B4406 by the Penmachno Mill SA (NS)

16 After 2 km (1½ miles) at T-j L, then at X-roads with A5 SA

17 Ignore 1st right after 800 m (½ mile) signed 'Siloam'. After further 1 km of climbing take the next R 'Nebo'

18 At X-roads (with B5427/B5113) by Give Way sign SA, then at T-j by next Give Way sign L

19 After 800 m (½ mile) on a sharp RH bend bear L (in effect SA) 'Single track road'

20 At fork on steep descent bear R. At T-j (with B5427) bear R

21 At T-j at the end of Nebo Road with a telephone box ahead R. At X-roads SA (or L for Llanrwst)

◀ page 27

⚠ Take care not to mistake the faded yellow line of the national park boundary for the solid yellow line of the route

Through the Clwyd Hills, north from Denbigh

One of two rides using Denbigh as a base. This ride starts from the top of the hill in Denbigh so be prepared for a final unwelcome climb right at the end of the ride! The first third of the ride is fairly flat with the exception of the Vale of Clwyd between Trefnant and Rhuallt. The route heads east then southeast, rising to over 198 m (650 ft) with fine views out to the Dee Estuary. Short sections of quiet lanes are stitched together to bring you to Nannerch and the longest climb of the day, right through the heart of the Clwyd Hills, which is not nearly as bad as you would imagine having spent most of the ride looking at the looming bulk of the range. The hills rise to over 548 m (1800 ft); the pass is at 289 m (950 ft), with less than 152 m (500 ft) climbing up from Nannerch. After a fast descent there is a flat, 5-km (3-mile) section across the Vale of Clwyd before that final climb up through Denbigh itself.

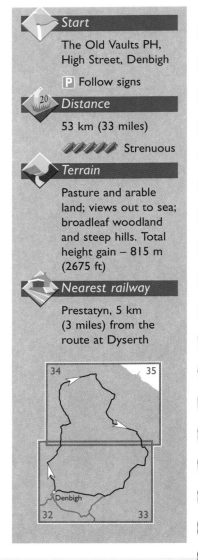

Start

The Old Vaults PH, High Street, Denbigh

P Follow signs

Distance

53 km (33 miles)

Strenuous

Terrain

Pasture and arable land; views out to sea; broadleaf woodland and steep hills. Total height gain – 815 m (2675 ft)

Nearest railway

Prestatyn, 5 km (3 miles) from the route at Dyserth

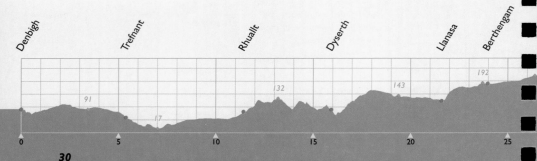

Denbigh 1

An ancient market town on a steep hillside overlooking the Vale of Clwyd. The medieval town walls are mostly intact. The castle, built in 1282 by Edward I, stands on a hill above the town. Eight towers and the gatehouse remain

St Asaph 3 km *(2 miles) north of the route at 2*

Britain's smallest cathedral stands on a hill beside the River Elwy, founded in AD 560 by St Kentigern, and rebuilt in the late 15th century. The village has a 14th-century parish church and 17th-century coaching inn

Bodrhyddan Hall *west of the route near 8*

Handsome, mainly 17th-century mansion. Superb display of 15th-century arms, armour and carved panels from a Spanish Armada galleon. The Egyptian collection includes an ancient mummy 3000 years old

▼ *Bwlch Penbarra, Clwydian Hills*

Refreshments

Plenty of choice in **Denbigh**
Farmers Arms PH, *between* **Trefnant** *and* **Rhuallt**
White House Hotel, Smithy Arms PH, **Rhualt**
Blue Lion PH 🍺, **Cwm**
Eagle & Child PH 🍺, **Gwaenysgor**
Red Lion PH, **Llanasa**
Black Lion PH, **Babell**
Cross & Foxes PH, **Nannerch**
Kinmel Arms PH, **Waen**

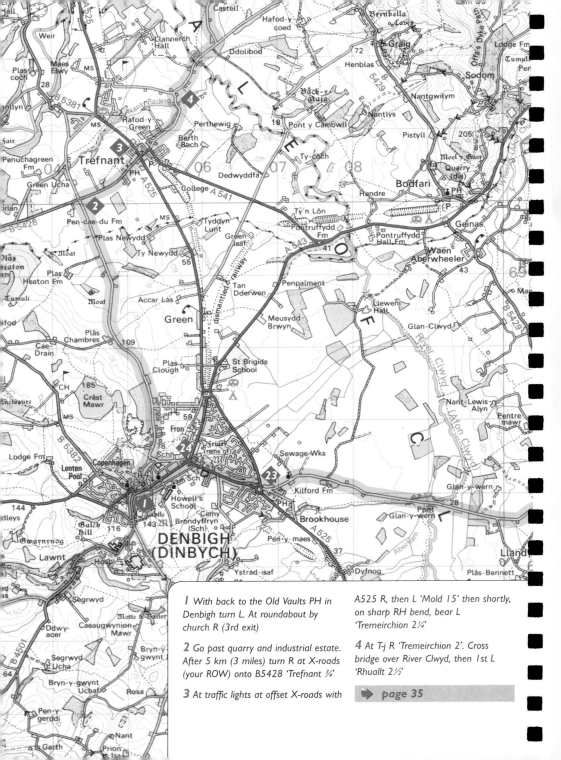

1 With back to the Old Vaults PH in Denbigh turn L. At roundabout by church R (3rd exit)

2 Go past quarry and industrial estate. After 5 km (3 miles) turn R at X-roads (your ROW) onto B5428 'Trefnant ¾'

3 At traffic lights at offset X-roads with A525 R, then L 'Mold 15' then shortly, on sharp RH bend, bear L 'Tremeirchion 2¼'

4 At T-j R 'Tremeirchion 2'. Cross bridge over River Clwyd, then 1st L 'Rhuallt 2½'

➡ page 35

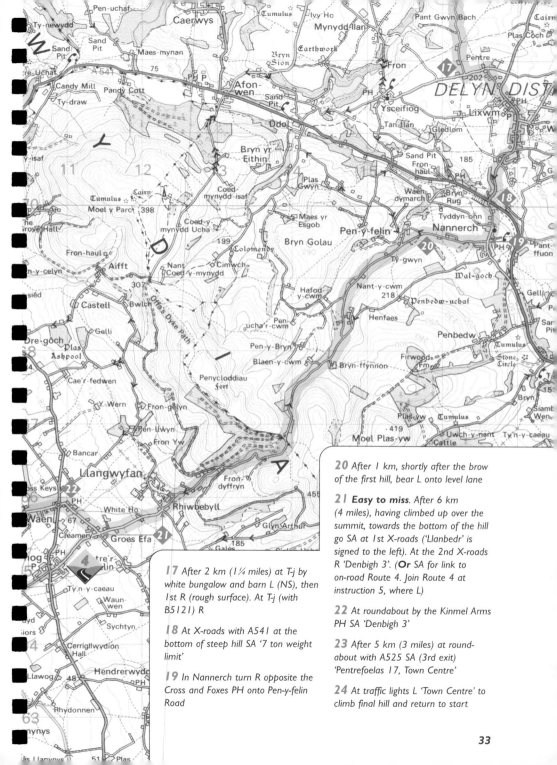

20 After 1 km, shortly after the brow of the first hill, bear L onto level lane

21 **Easy to miss**. After 6 km (4 miles), having climbed up over the summit, towards the bottom of the hill go SA at 1st X-roads ('Llanbedr' is signed to the left). At the 2nd X-roads R 'Denbigh 3'. (**Or** SA for link to on-road Route 4. Join Route 4 at instruction 5, where L)

22 At roundabout by the Kinmel Arms PH SA 'Denbigh 3'

23 After 5 km (3 miles) at round-about with A525 SA (3rd exit) 'Pentrefoelas 17, Town Centre'

24 At traffic lights L 'Town Centre' to climb final hill and return to start

17 After 2 km (1¼ miles) at T-j by white bungalow and barn L (NS), then 1st R (rough surface). At T-j (with B5121) R

18 At X-roads with A541 at the bottom of steep hill SA '7 ton weight limit'

19 In Nannerch turn R opposite the Cross and Foxes PH onto Pen-y-felin Road

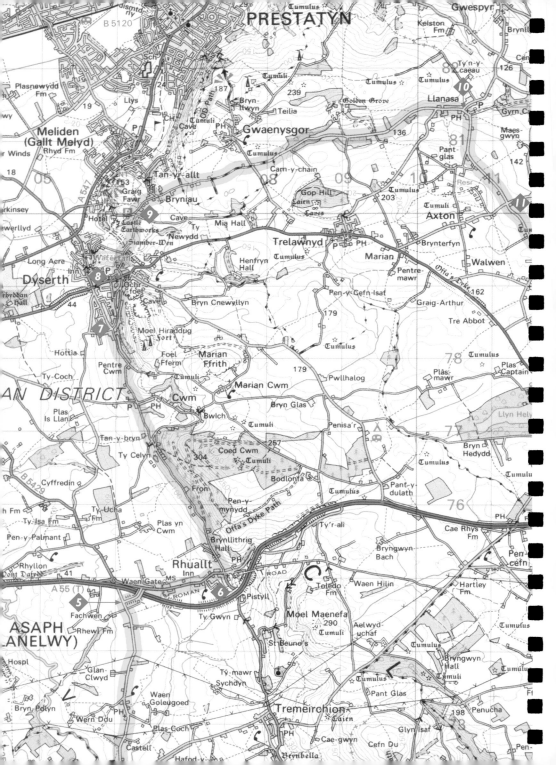

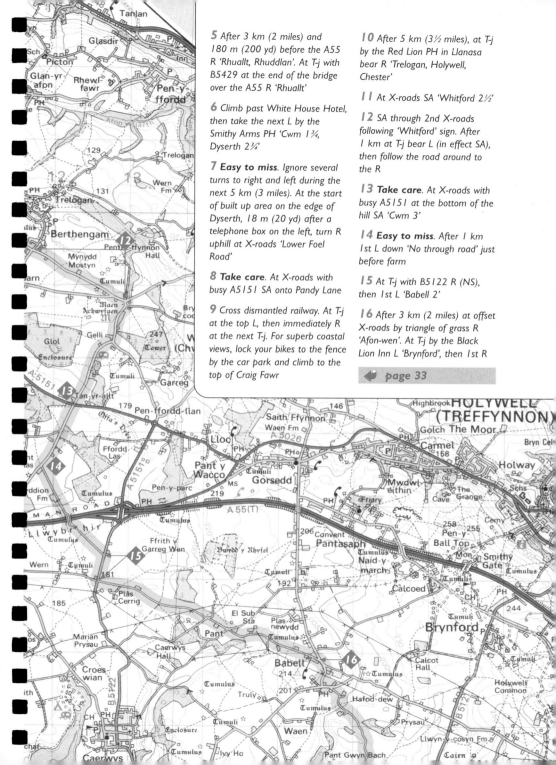

5 After 3 km (2 miles) and 180 m (200 yd) before the A55 R 'Rhuallt, Rhuddlan'. At T-j with B5429 at the end of the bridge over the A55 R 'Rhuallt'

6 Climb past White House Hotel, then take the next L by the Smithy Arms PH 'Cwm 1¾, Dyserth 2¾'

7 **Easy to miss**. Ignore several turns to right and left during the next 5 km (3 miles). At the start of built up area on the edge of Dyserth, 18 m (20 yd) after a telephone box on the left, turn R uphill at X-roads 'Lower Foel Road'

8 **Take care**. At X-roads with busy A5151 SA onto Pandy Lane

9 Cross dismantled railway. At T-j at the top L, then immediately R at the next T-j. For superb coastal views, lock your bikes to the fence by the car park and climb to the top of Craig Fawr

10 After 5 km (3½ miles), at T-j by the Red Lion PH in Llanasa bear R 'Trelogan, Holywell, Chester'

11 At X-roads SA 'Whitford 2½'

12 SA through 2nd X-roads following 'Whitford' sign. After 1 km at T-j bear L (in effect SA), then follow the road around to the R

13 **Take care**. At X-roads with busy A5151 at the bottom of the hill SA 'Cwm 3'

14 **Easy to miss**. After 1 km 1st L down 'No through road' just before farm

15 At T-j with B5122 R (NS), then 1st L 'Babell 2'

16 After 3 km (2 miles) at offset X-roads by triangle of grass R 'Afon-wen'. At T-j by the Black Lion Inn L 'Brynford', then 1st R

◄ page 33

Hills, forests and reservoirs, southwest of Denbigh

The quiet, flat lanes through the Vale of Clwyd between Pentre-Llanrhaeadr and Ruthin would be suitable for the most reluctant of cyclists, however, the route west of Ruthin will tax the muscles of the fittest. The ridge between the valleys of the rivers Clwyd and Clywedog is crossed and the wooded valley of the latter is followed from Bontuchel to Cyffylliog – your last chance of refreshment for several kilometres. A climb of over 274 m (900 ft) takes you up a spur from Cyffylliog, into the fields, then onwards and upwards to the first high point of the ride near the crossroads at instruction 16. A fast and furious descent to cross Afon Alwen to the south of the Llyn Brenig Reservoir is followed by a steady climb back up to 427 m (1400 ft). Once out of the forestry the fun really begins with a superb descent on a narrow road with magnificent views ahead. A last climb brings you back past the castle to return to the start.

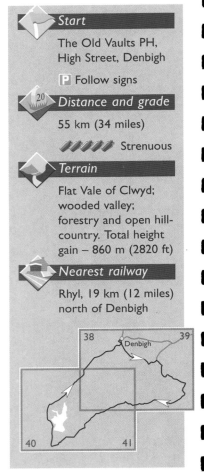

Start

The Old Vaults PH, High Street, Denbigh

P Follow signs

Distance and grade

55 km (34 miles)

///// Strenuous

Terrain

Flat Vale of Clwyd; wooded valley; forestry and open hill-country. Total height gain – 860 m (2820 ft)

Nearest railway

Rhyl, 19 km (12 miles) north of Denbigh

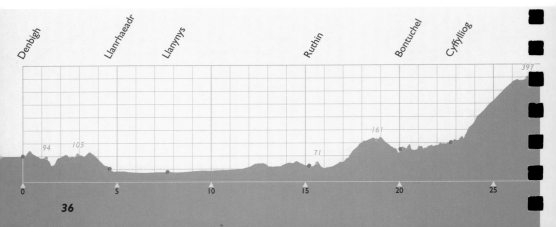

 **Places of interest**

Ruthin 11

The town boasts a mixture of Medieval, Tudor, Georgian, Regency and Victorian buildings. St Peter's Church has a carved oak roof, said to be the gift of Henry VII

Clocaenog Forest 16

Mixed woodland of 6,070 ha (15,000 acres), replanted in 1930-34, on high moorland, enclosing Alwen and Llyn Brenig reservoirs

Llyn Brenig 18

Reservoir of 370 ha (919 acres) in two valleys high on Mynydd Hiraethog. Visitor centre, nature and archaeological trails

▼ *Clocaenog Forest*

Refreshments

Plenty of choice in **Denbigh**
Kings Head PH 🍺, **Llanrhaeadr**
Y Cwmro Inn, **Pentre Llanrhaeadr**
Cerigllwydian Arms PH 🍺🍺, **Llanynys**
Drovers Arms PH 🍺, **Rhewl** (just off the route near 6)
Olde Anchor PH 🍺, *plenty of choice in* **Ruthin**
Old Cross Keys PH, **Llanfwrog**
Bridge Hotel, **Bontuchel**
Red Lion Hotel, **Cyffylliog**

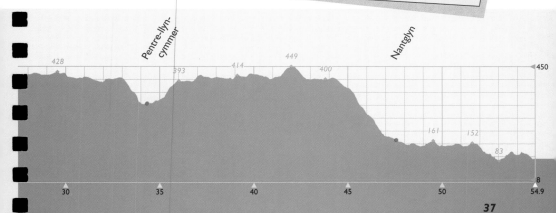

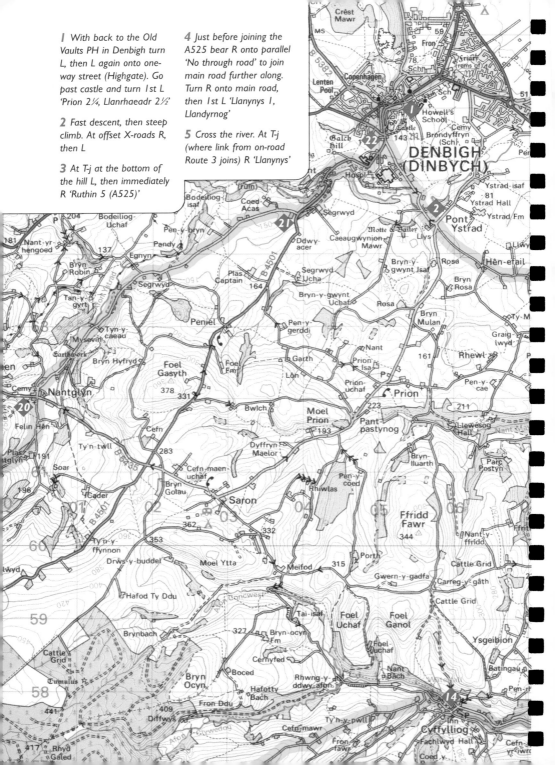

1 With back to the Old Vaults PH in Denbigh turn L, then L again onto one-way street (Highgate). Go past castle and turn 1st L 'Prion 2¼, Llanrhaeadr 2½'

2 Fast descent, then steep climb. At offset X-roads R, then L

3 At T-j at the bottom of the hill L, then immediately R 'Ruthin 5 (A525)'

4 Just before joining the A525 bear R onto parallel 'No through road' to join main road further along. Turn R onto main road, then 1st L 'Llanynys 1, Llandyrnog'

5 Cross the river. At T-j (where link from on-road Route 3 joins) R 'Llanynys'

6 Go past Cerrigllwydian Arms. **Easy to miss**. 2 km (1¼ miles) after the pub 1st L (NS)

7 At T-j by triangle of grass R 'Ruthin'. After 1 km on sharp RH bend bear L (in effect SA) then shortly, at the next T-j L

8 Cross bridge over river, then 1st R

9 At T-j (with B5429) by large brick house with conservatory R then shortly, 1st R at X-roads

10 At T-j with main road after the start of the built-up area R, then at the roundabout 2nd exit L 'Town Centre'

11 At roundabout/main square in Ruthin SA and slightly R onto Clwyd Street 'Denbigh (A525)'

12 At T-j with A494 by the Park Place Hotel bear L (in effect SA) 'Bala'

13 Continue SA on this road as it becomes the B5105 ('Cerrigydrudion'). Shortly after passing the church and the Old Cross Keys PH, next R 'Bontuchel 1¾, Cyffylliog 3'

14 Climb, then descend. Lovely river section. In Cyffylliog, just before the Red Lion Hotel, turn R 'Nantglyn', then 1st L 'Pentre-llyn-cymmer 6'

⇨ page 40

20 Superb descent. The surface of the road is at times rough. Through Nantglyn following signs for Denbigh

21 Short climb. At T-j with B4501 L 'Denbigh 1½'

22 Just before the castle L onto one way system 'Town Centre ¾'. At T-j R 'Town Centre' to return to the start

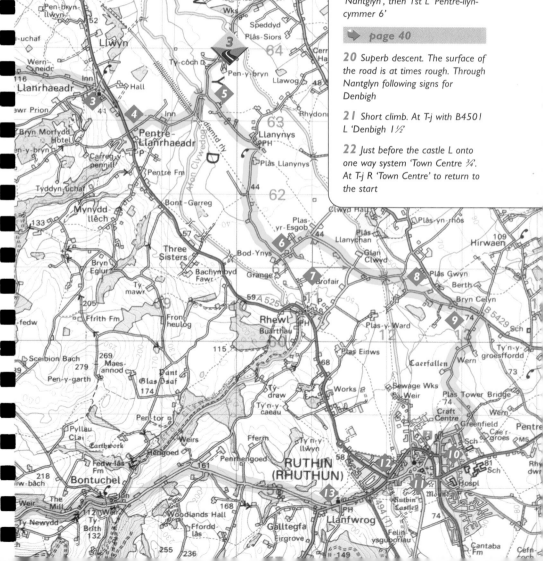

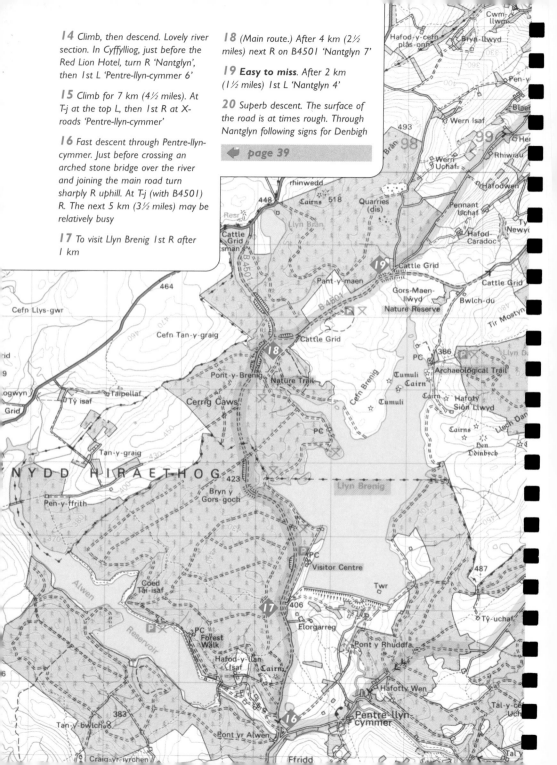

14 *Climb, then descend. Lovely river section. In Cyffylliog, just before the Red Lion Hotel, turn R 'Nantglyn', then 1st L 'Pentre-llyn-cymmer 6'*

15 *Climb for 7 km (4½ miles). At T-j at the top L, then 1st R at X-roads 'Pentre-llyn-cymmer'*

16 *Fast descent through Pentre-llyn-cymmer. Just before crossing an arched stone bridge over the river and joining the main road turn sharply R uphill. At T-j (with B4501) R. The next 5 km (3½ miles) may be relatively busy*

17 *To visit Llyn Brenig 1st R after 1 km*

18 *(Main route.) After 4 km (2½ miles) next R on B4501 'Nantglyn 7'*

19 Easy to miss. *After 2 km (1½ miles) 1st L 'Nantglyn 4'*

20 *Superb descent. The surface of the road is at times rough. Through Nantglyn following signs for Denbigh*

◀ **page 39**

5 Lakes and passes in the Berwyn Mountains

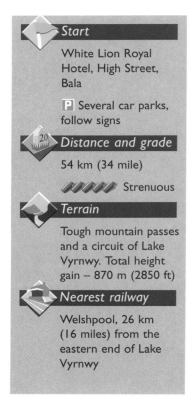

Start

White Lion Royal Hotel, High Street, Bala

P Several car parks, follow signs

Distance and grade

54 km (34 mile)

Strenuous

Terrain

Tough mountain passes and a circuit of Lake Vyrnwy. Total height gain – 870 m (2850 ft)

Nearest railway

Welshpool, 26 km (16 miles) from the eastern end of Lake Vyrnwy

With its two lakes and two challenging mountain passes there is something simple and symmetrical about this tough ride into the Berwyn Mountains. From Bala the ridge between Bala Lake and the valley of Cwm Hirnant is soon crossed and the first long climb begins. This passes alongside a stream, through forestry, before emerging into bleak, open moorland and climbing to over 488 m (1600 ft). The descent is shorter than the climb as Lake Vyrnwy is over 90 m (300 ft) higher than Lake Bala. The circuit of Lake Vyrnwy is one of the few flat rides in the region – appropriate for gentle leisure cycling and families. After the gentle circuit of the lake prepare for the climb to the top of the highest road in Wales – Bwlch y Groes at 546 m (1792 ft). In a reverse of the outward leg the climb is shorter than the descent which drops you close to the southwest end of Lake Bala. It is best to leave this ride until a day of good visibility as the views from the summits of the two passes are spectacular.

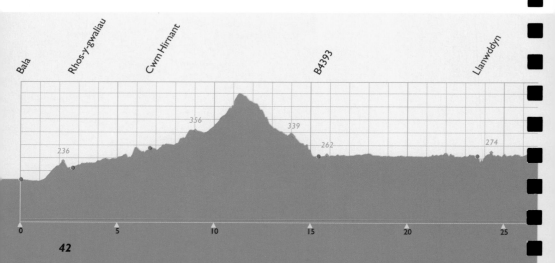

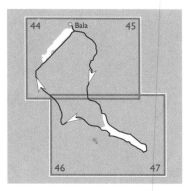

44 ○ Bala 45

46 47

Refreshments

Olde Bulls Head PH 🍺, *Ship Inn* 🍺, *plenty of choice in* **Bala**
Coffees and Tavern Bar, Lake Vyrnwy Hotel, west end of **Lake Vyrnwy**

▼ Bwlch y Groes, Pennant Valley

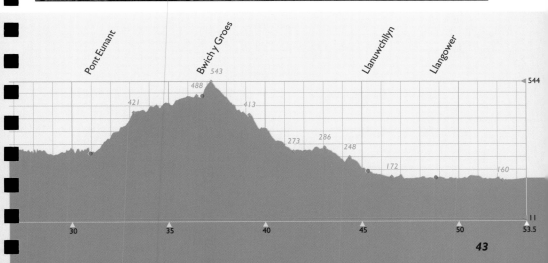

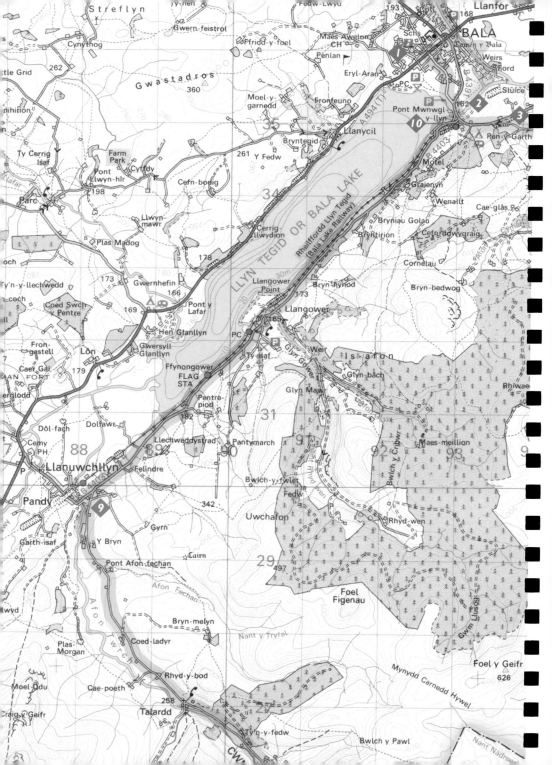

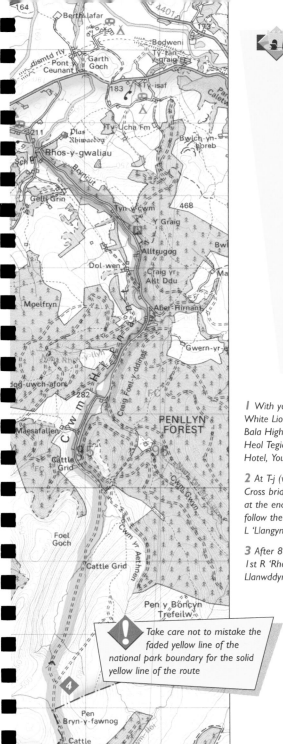

Places of interest

Bala I

The town, which basically consists of one, long, tree-lined street of shops, inns and eating places, is traditionally Welsh in tone and temperament. The scene is set by a statue of the Liberal MP and advocate of home rule for Wales, Thomas Edward Ellis (1859-99) in suitably flamboyant pose

Bala Lake I

The largest natural lake in Wales, 7 km (4 miles) long, over 1 km wide and 46 m (150 ft) deep. It is the only home of the trout-like gwyniad and the site of a legendary drowned palace. A lakeside steam railway runs between the town of Bala and Llanuwchllyn

1 With your back to the White Lion Royal Hotel in Bala High Street SA onto Heol Tegid 'Bala Lake Hotel, Youth Hostel'

2 At T-j (with B4391) R. Cross bridge over the river at the end of the lake and follow the road round to the L 'Llangynog'

3 After 800 m (½ mile) 1st R 'Rhos-y-gwaliau, Llyn Llanwddyn, Lake Vyrnwy'

4 Ignore turnings to right and left. Cross stream and climb for 6 miles to the highpoint of this section at 500 m (1640 ft). Over the summit and descend for 3 km (2 miles)

➡ page 46

9 8-km (5-mile) descent. At T-j with B4403 at the bottom of the hill R

10 At T-j with B4391 L 'Bala', then 1st L to return to the start

! Take care not to mistake the faded yellow line of the national park boundary for the solid yellow line of the route

Take care not to mistake the faded yellow line of the national park boundary for the solid yellow line of the route

▲ Lake Vyrnwy

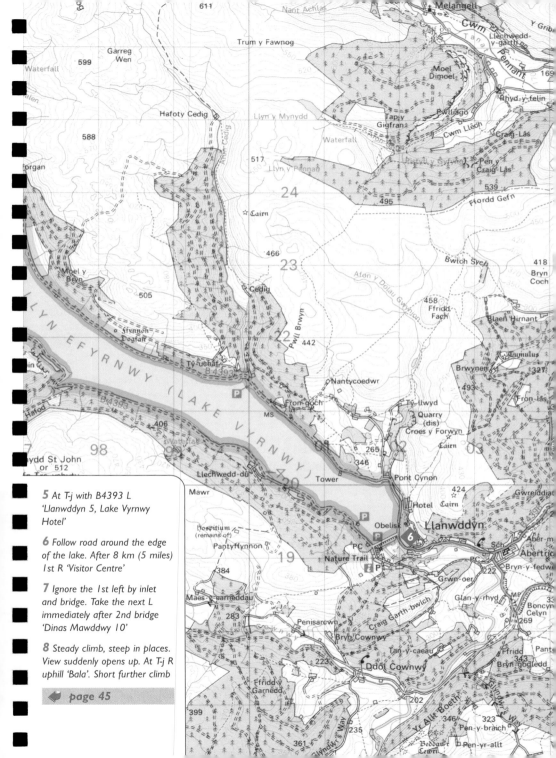

5 *At T-j with B4393 L 'Llanwddyn 5, Lake Vyrnwy Hotel'*

6 *Follow road around the edge of the lake. After 8 km (5 miles) 1st R 'Visitor Centre'*

7 *Ignore the 1st left by inlet and bridge. Take the next L immediately after 2nd bridge 'Dinas Mawddwy 10'*

8 *Steady climb, steep in places. View suddenly opens up. At T-j R uphill 'Bala'. Short further climb*

Along the Ceiriog Valley, west of Oswestry

The quietest exit from Oswestry takes you past the Iron Age hill fort, north to Weston Rhyn, from where you climb then drop into the steep, wooded valley formed by the Ceiriog River. There are views across the valley to Chirk Castle and you will pass some curious man-made caves cut into the rock to your left. Between Chirk and Glyn Ceiriog the route continues on minor roads parallel to the busy B4500 but beyond this there are few settlements and the road is much quieter. Llanarmon Dyffryn Ceiriog seems in many ways the end of the line but a narrow mountain road climbs steeply into the Berwyn Mountains with the fine all-round views one has a right to expect after climbing to 427 m (1400 ft). Offa's Dyke Path, the long-distance footpath from Chepstow to Prestatyn, is crossed a second time near to Croesau Bach on the return to Oswestry.

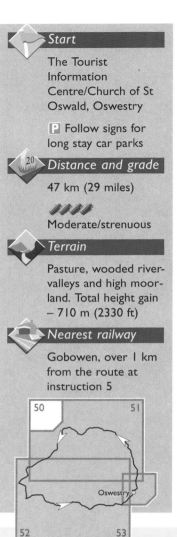

Start

The Tourist Information Centre/Church of St Oswald, Oswestry

P Follow signs for long stay car parks

Distance and grade

47 km (29 miles)

Moderate/strenuous

Terrain

Pasture, wooded river-valleys and high moor-land. Total height gain – 710 m (2330 ft)

Nearest railway

Gobowen, over 1 km from the route at instruction 5

Oswestry 1

Welsh border town with several timber-framed houses lining the main street: the 17th-century Llwyd Mansion, Fox Inn and Coach & Dogs Inn. St Oswald's Church dates from the 13th century. Oswestry's one-way system and pedestrianised centre means that the town itself is best explored on foot before or after the ride

Chirk over 1 km north of the route near 6

A village set in a woodland, mountain and river landscape. The nearby castle, built by Edward I in the late 13th century, is still occupied and has been the home of the Myddleton family since the end of the 16th century. Elaborate 18th-century iron gates with ornamental faces lead to 180 ha (460 acres) of wooded parkland

Ceiriog Valley over 1 km north of the route near 5

Contains two graceful examples of 19th-century civil engineering: Thomas Telford's aqueduct, completed in 1801, carrying the Llangollen Canal 21 m (70 ft) above the river – overlooked by an impressive railway viaduct – in use since 1848

▲ Old tram, Glyn Ceirios Museum, Wrexham

Refreshments

Fox PH 🍺, plenty of choice in **Oswestry**
The Lodge PH, **Weston Rhyn**
Golden Pheasant PH 🍺, **Llwynmawr, just east of Glyn Ceiriog**
Glyn Valley Hotel, Royal Oak PH, **Glyn Ceiriog**
Woolpack Inn, **Pandy**
West Arms PH 🍺, Hand PH 🍺, **Llanarmon Dyffryn Ceiriog**
Wynnstay PH 🍺, **Llansilin**

Llanarmon Dyffryn Ceiriog — 420
313
342
Moelfre
216
Llansilin
164 — 159
Croesau Bach
282
150
421
109

25   30   35   40   45   47.0

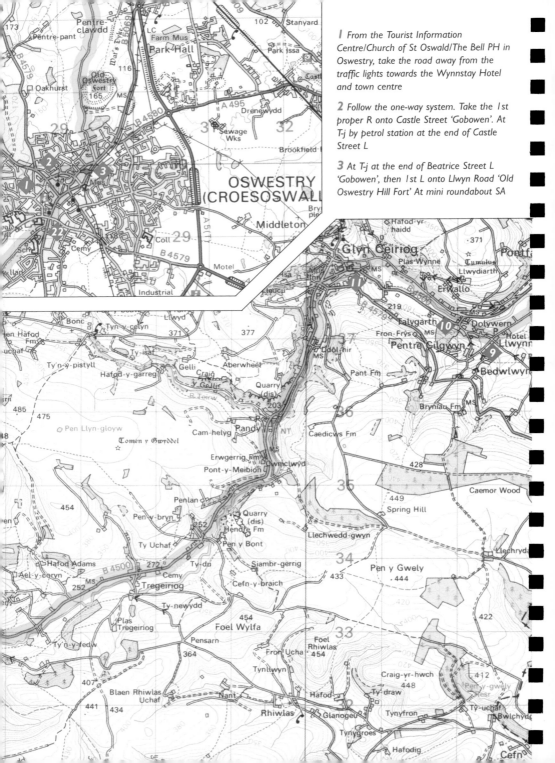

1 *From the Tourist Information Centre/Church of St Oswald/The Bell PH in Oswestry, take the road away from the traffic lights towards the Wynnstay Hotel and town centre*

2 *Follow the one-way system. Take the 1st proper R onto Castle Street 'Gobowen'. At T-j by petrol station at the end of Castle Street L*

3 *At T-j at the end of Beatrice Street L 'Gobowen', then 1st L onto Llwyn Road 'Old Oswestry Hill Fort' At mini roundabout SA*

4 At T-j by triangle of grass L (NS). At X-roads by Give Way sign SA 'Weston Rhyn'

5 Continue SA at two X-roads (your ROW)

6 At T-j R 'Weston Rhyn'. At mini-roundabout by the Lodge PH in Weston Rhyn 1st exit L 'Quinta ¼, Bronygarth 1½'

7 Past man-made stone caves to the left. Cross Offa's Dyke Path. At fork of roads by letter box take the LH upper lane

8 Ignore left and right turns, following the lane in the same direction, climbing then descending. At T-j at the bottom of the hill by a Give Way sign L (NS)

9 At X-roads by the Golden Pheasant Hotel R 'Glyn Ceiriog 1½'

10 At T-j with more major road R, then L immediately after the bridge

11 At T-j with B4500 R 'Llanarmon DC 5'. Through Glyn Ceiriog following signs for Llanarmon DC

➡ **page 52**

22 At T-j (with B5069) at the end of Pen-y-llan Lane with the Golden Lion PH ahead, turn L. At traffic lights, SA to return to the start

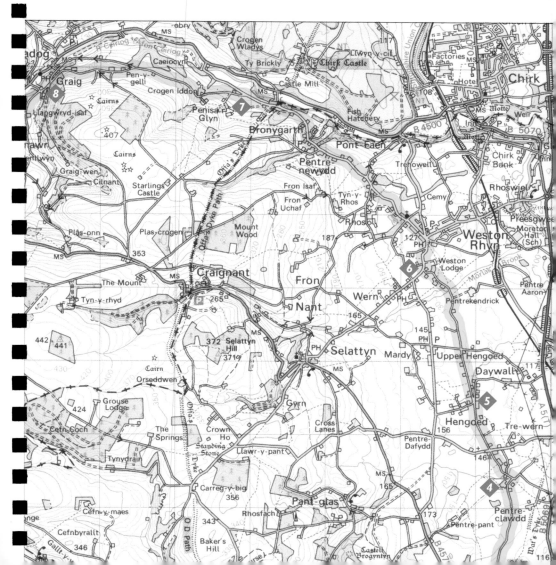

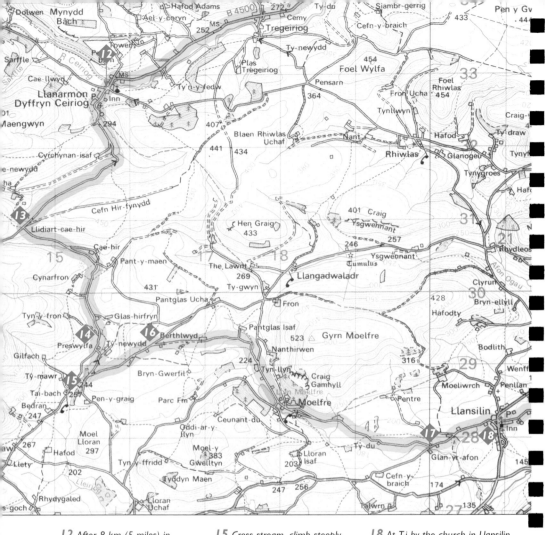

12 After 8 km (5 miles) in Llanarmon continue SA following signs for Llanrhaeadr

13 Long, steep climb. At the junction, shortly after the top of the hill, follow the road round to the L 'Llanrhaeadr YM'

14 *Easy to miss*. After 2 km (1½ miles) of descent, by a triangle of grass with a tree to your left, turn L downhill 'Efail-rhyd'

15 Cross stream, climb steeply, 1st L sharply back on yourself immediately after a small building (chapel)

16 At fork of roads, shortly after the brow of the hill, take the RH, lower lane. Go through two gates (the road surface on the section between the gates may be rough)

17 Continue downhill past lake and follow signs for Llansilin. At T-j by letter box L 'Llansilin'

18 At T-j by the church in Llansilin L, then 1st R

19 At T-j at the top of the hill by small triangle of grass L

20 At T-j after 3 km (2 miles) L 'Oswestry', then after 27 m (300 yd) 1st R '2 ton weight limit'

21 After 800 m (½ mile) 1st L on Pen-y-llan Lane 'Unsuitable for HGVs'

◀ page 51

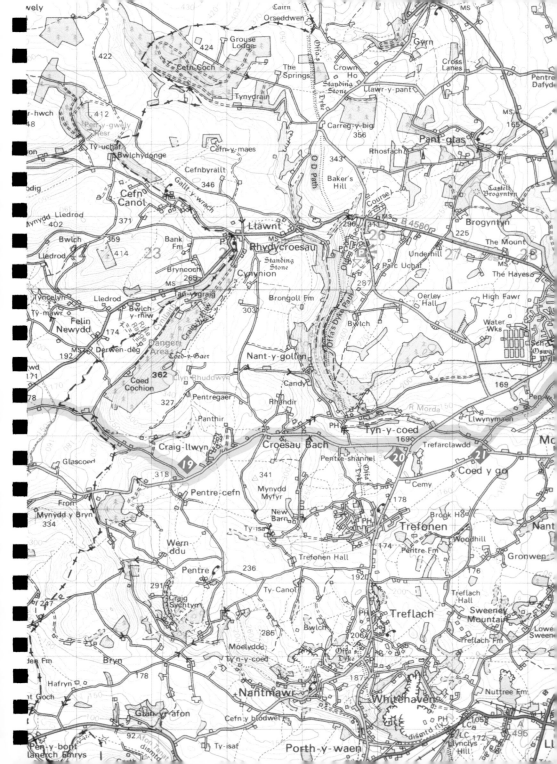

Through the Cheshire Plain around Whitchurch

This is the easiest on-road ride in the book: the longest climb, out of the valley to the south of Malpas, amounts to little over 30 m (100 ft). The ride is situated in the Cheshire Plain: the wide expanse of fertile land between the Welsh hills beyond Wrexham and Oswestry to the west and the Peak District to the east. There are hundreds of kilometres of quiet lanes to explore, many linked by the county-wide route known as the Cheshire Cycleway. From the start at Whitchurch the route takes a narrow lane out to the charming village of Marbury with its fine old black and white timbered lodge, its lake and excellent hostelry. The route continues west to Malpas before turning south to that one noticeable hill of the ride – in and out of the valley of Wych Brook. South of the A495 the Shropshire Union Canal is crossed for the second time and is roughly followed all the way back to Whitchurch as you climb to the highest point of the ride at a dizzying 129 m (423 ft)!

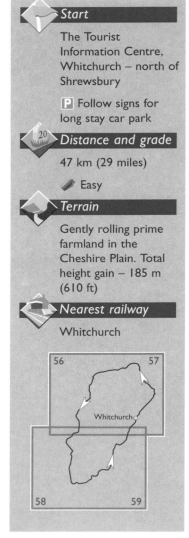

Start

The Tourist Information Centre, Whitchurch – north of Shrewsbury

P Follow signs for long stay car park

Distance and grade

47 km (29 miles)

Easy

Terrain

Gently rolling prime farmland in the Cheshire Plain. Total height gain – 185 m (610 ft)

Nearest railway

Whitchurch

▶ Cheshire Plain

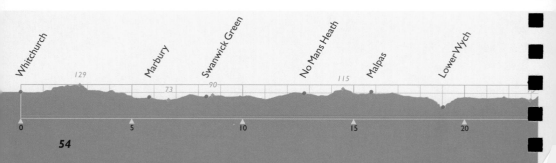

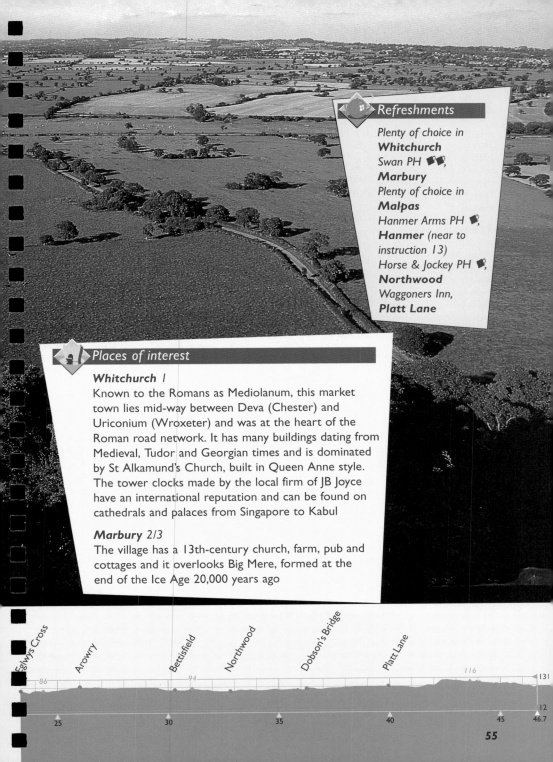

Refreshments

Plenty of choice in
Whitchurch
Swan PH,
Marbury
Plenty of choice in
Malpas
Hanmer Arms PH,
Hanmer (near to
instruction 13)
Horse & Jockey PH,
Northwood
Waggoners Inn,
Platt Lane

Places of interest

Whitchurch 1

Known to the Romans as Mediolanum, this market
town lies mid-way between Deva (Chester) and
Uriconium (Wroxeter) and was at the heart of the
Roman road network. It has many buildings dating from
Medieval, Tudor and Georgian times and is dominated
by St Alkamund's Church, built in Queen Anne style.
The tower clocks made by the local firm of JB Joyce
have an international reputation and can be found on
cathedrals and palaces from Singapore to Kabul

Marbury 2/3

The village has a 13th-century church, farm, pub and
cottages and it overlooks Big Mere, formed at the
end of the Ice Age 20,000 years ago

Eglwys Cross
Arowry
Betrisfield
Northwood
Dobson's Bridge
Platt Lane

86   94   116   131
25   30   35   40   45   46.7   12

1 With back to the Tourist Information Centre in Whitchurch R. At T-j at the end of the High Street by large church and Black Bear PH R towards Horse & Jockey PH

2 Ignore 1st L ('No Entry'). Take 2nd L on St John's Street. At T-j at the end of St John's Street L, then 1st R onto Claypit Street 'Wirswall 2, Marbury 4'

3 Follow this road for 10 km (6 miles), passing through Marbury following signs for Bickley. **Easy to miss**. Cross the canal. Ignore two right turns. Shortly after passing a pair of black and white timbered houses on your left, take the next R on a sharp LH bend (NS)

4 At X-roads with the A49 SA 'Bickley Church ½, No Mans Heath 2, Malpas 4'

5 If you wish to visit Cholmondeley Castle take the 2nd R 'Bickerton, Bickley Church'. For continuation of route go SA

6 **Take care**. At offset X-roads with busy A41 SA on to Cross o' th' Hill Road 'Malpas 2'

7 Follow one-way system in Malpas. At T-j R for refreshments and the fine old buildings of Malpas or L to continue route

8 Follow signs for Whitchurch out of Malpas. Shortly, at the edge of the village, 1st R 'Old Castle'

9 **Easy to miss**. After 1 km, 1st L

10 Follow this lane for 6 km (4 miles), ignoring turns to right and left, dipping into the Wych Valley and climbing the only steep hill of the whole ride

11 At the offset X-roads with the A525 R, then L 'Arowry 1½'

12 At offset X-roads by double triangle of grass 1st R 'Arowry 1, Hanmer 1¼'

➡ page 58

18 After 8 km (5 miles) at X-roads in Whitchurch at the end of Alkington Road SA onto Bark Hill. At T-j at the end of Bark Hill L, then at roundabout R 'No cars or motorbikes'. At T-j by ornate clock L to return to the start

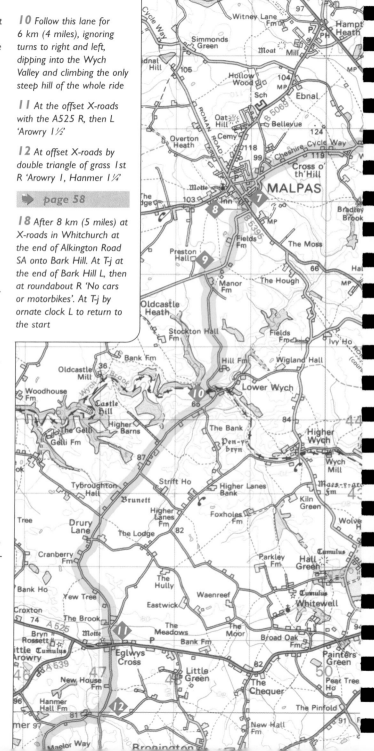

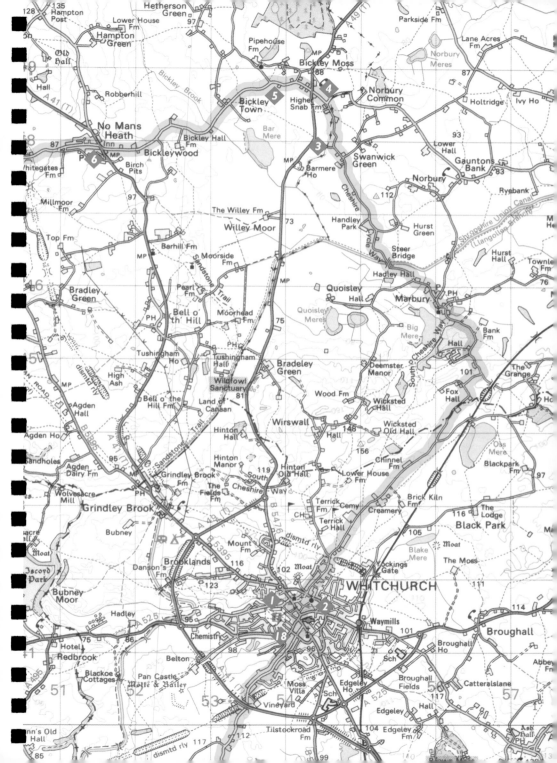

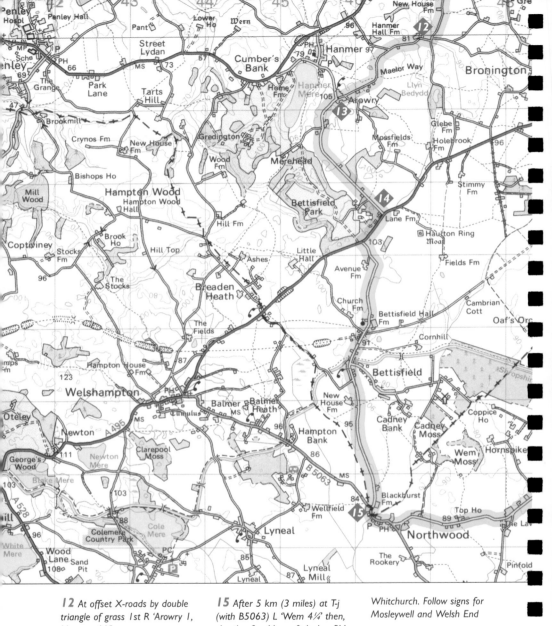

12 At offset X-roads by double triangle of grass 1st R 'Arowry 1, Hanmer 1¼'

13 At T-j L 'Ellesmere 6'

14 At T-j with A495 R 'Ellesmere 5, Oswestry 13', then 1st L 'Bettisfield 1, Wem 7'

15 After 5 km (3 miles) at T-j (with B5063) L 'Wem 4¼' then, shortly after Horse & Jockey PH, next L 'Whixall 2, Prees 7'

16 Go past red brick church, cross bridge over canal, ignore right turn to Bostock Hall and

Whitchurch. Follow signs for Mosleywell and Welsh End

17 At X-roads by Waggoners Inn SA 'Whitchurch'

← page 56

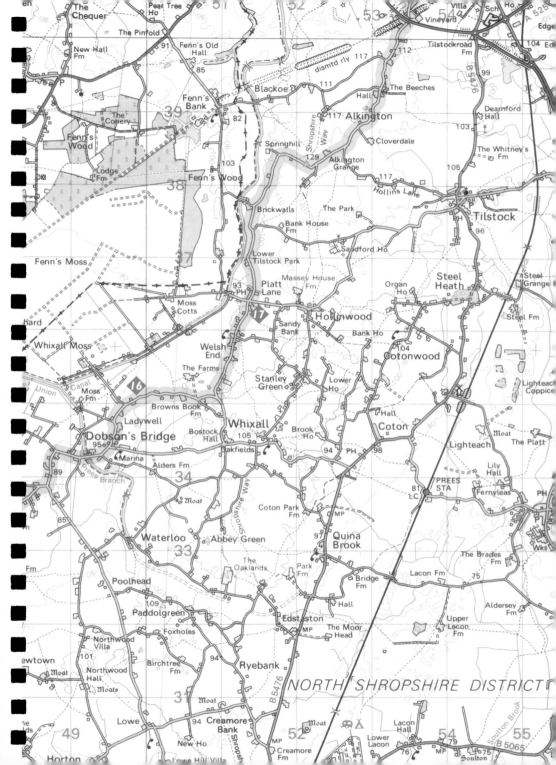

Into the hills above the Dovey Valley from Machynlleth

8

Start

The clocktower, Machynlleth, on the A487 north of Aberystwyth

P Follow signs

Distance and grade

61 km (38 miles)

Strenuous

Terrain

River valleys; broadleaf woodland; forestry plantations and a high mountain pass. Total height gain – 1100 m (3610 ft)

Nearest railway

Machynlleth

Three of the busiest trunk roads in Mid-Wales meet near Machynlleth but luckily there are quiet lanes running parallel to them for all but short sections. The first such short (and busy) section is at the very start of the ride, as you have to cross the River Dovey, north of Machynlleth. The route continues north along the lovely Dulas Valley as far as the slate mines of Aberllefenni before turning east, climbing steeply through Dyfi Forest, then dropping back down into the Dovey Valley for a second, delightful river section. The wind farms beckon from the hills ahead. South of the A470 you climb steadily, first on the B4518 then west on the mountain road, past the spectacular Dylife Gorge, to the panoramic views from the summit of the pass at 509 m (1670 ft). It is well worth leaving this ride until a day of good visibility. Whatever the weather the descent back to Machynlleth should bring a grin to the most tired of cyclists!

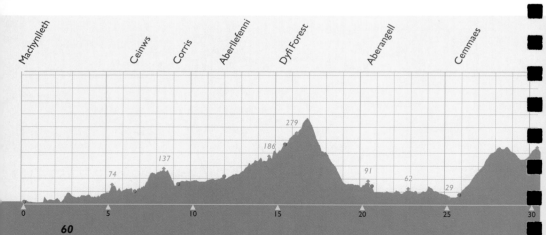

Machynlleth 1

The Victorian Gothic clocktower with pinnacles, spires and a four-faced clock straddles the main street. The building in Maengwyn Street stands on the site of the first Welsh parliament held by the rebel leader Owain Glyndwr in 1404. There is an exhibition devoted to Owain's life and times

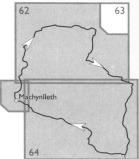

62	63
Machynlleth	
64	

Corris 5

A village of narrow streets and dark-stoned terraces topped with slate roofs and hemmed in by thick forests and steep mountain slopes. Slate is the key to Corris's past – the village grew up alongside its slate quarries, which flourished in the second half of the 19th century when 1000 men were employed here

▼ Victorian Gothic clocktower, Machynlleth

Refreshments

White Lion PH 🍺, plenty of choice in **Machynlleth**
Tafarn Dwynant PH, **Ceinwys**
Slaters Arms PH, tea shop, **Corris**
Penrhos Arms PH, **Cemmaes**
Wynnstay Arms PH 🍺, **Llanbrynmair**
Star Inn, **Dylife**

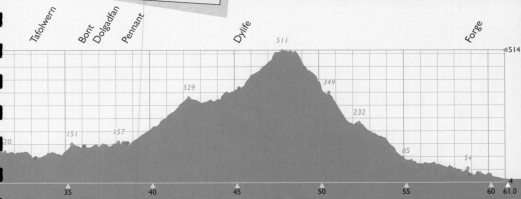

Tafolwern Bont Dolgadfan Pennant Dylife Forge

511
514
329
349
232
151 157
85
54
20
4
35 40 45 50 55 60 61.0

1 From the clock tower in Machynlleth take the A487 downhill towards Dolgellau

2 Under the railway bridge, over the river bridge following signs for 'Dollgellau'. 1 km after the river bridge 1st R onto B4404 'Llanwrin', then 1st L immediately after bridge 'Centre for Alternative Technology'

3 At T-j L, then immediately R at next T-j 'Bike Route 8'

4 Through Ceinws. Ignore several turns to the right. Immediately before the bridge near the main road bear R (in effect SA) onto lane parallel with the river

5 At X-roads by Slaters Arms PH in Corris turn R

6 Follow for 3 km (2 miles). After the slate factory in Aberllefenni, follow the road sharply to the R 'Aberangell',

7 Climb for 5 km (3½ miles), then descend for 5 km (3 miles) through forestry. After steep downhill section, cross bridge and cattle grid and follow the road round to the R

Take care not to mistake the faded yellow line of the national park boundary for the solid yellow line of the route

8 At T-j by triangle of grass and telephone box, past the stores in Aberangell, turn R

9 *Easy to miss.* After 3 km (2 miles) the road climbs away from the river. On a long, gentle descent take the 1st road to the L sharply back on yourself to cross bridge over River Dovey

10 At T-j (with A470) L, then R

11 Steep climb. **Easy to miss.** Shortly after passing left turn to Cemmaes Wind Farm, on a sharp RH bend, take the next L towards the wind turbines and follow signs for Llanbrynmair

12 After 5 km (3 miles) at T-j (with A470) L. **Take care** on next section: this is a busy road with a difficult right turn. After about 1 km, and immediately after crossing the railway bridge 1st R 'Tafolwern ½'. If you are concerned about the traffic, cross the bridge, continue past the turning, cross the road where the visibility is better and return to this point

➡ page 64

16 Wonderful descent over 4½ miles. Fairly flat river section, then final short climb between Forge and Machynlleth. At T-j with A489 on the outskirts of Machynlleth L to return to the clock tower

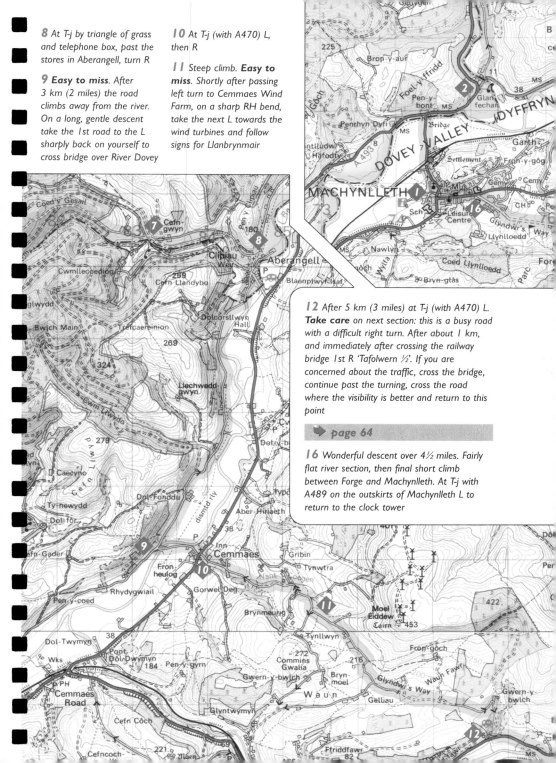

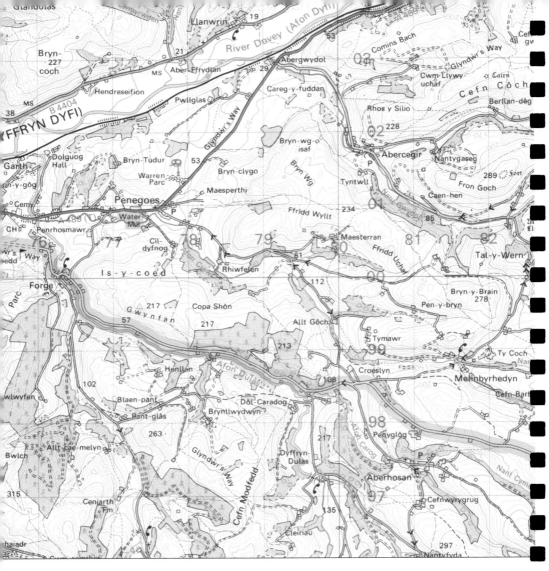

12 *After 5 km (3 miles) at T-j (with A470) L. **Take care** on next section: this is a busy road with a difficult right turn. After 1 km, and immediately after crossing the railway bridge 1st R 'Tafolwern ½'. If you are concerned about the traffic, cross the bridge, continue past the turning, cross the road where the visibility is better and return to this point*

13 *After 800 m (½ mile), just past the telephone box follow the road round to the L. At T-j (with B4518) R*

14 *Climb 200 m (650 ft) over 9 km (5½ miles). Shortly after the highest point, on descent 1st R 'Machynlleth 11, Forge 10, Dylife 1'. (**Or** for link to on-road Route 10 stay on B4518 for*

further 2 km (1¼ miles). Immediately after a 'No through road' to the right take the next R 'Llwynygog' to join Route 10 at instruction 9)

15 *Climb further 200 m (650 ft) over 5 km (3½ miles), passing the viewpoint for Dylife Gorge*

◀ page 63

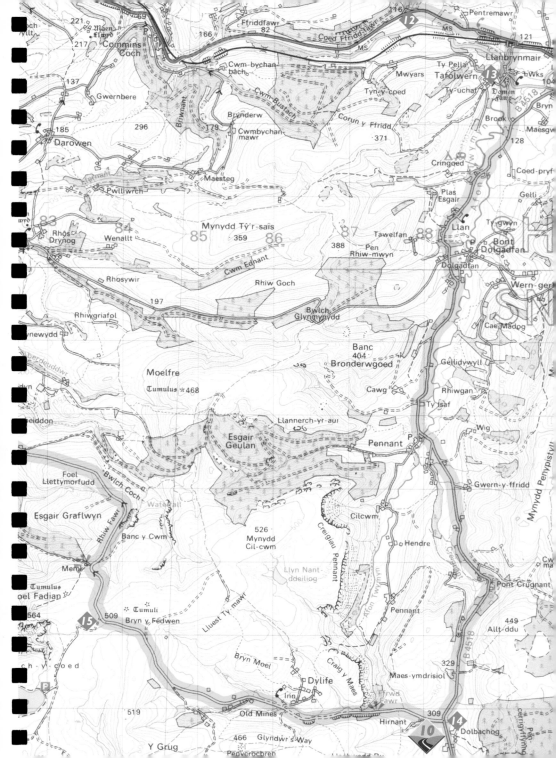

Hills and reservoirs, east of Aberystwyth

There are no flat, quiet routes out of Aberystwyth so do not be deterred by the climb out of town on the busy A487 as it is totally unrepresentative of the route that follows. (If you arrive by car there is an alternative starting point which avoids the town centre altogether.) As soon as you leave the A487 quiet lanes take you to the attractive village green in Tal-y-bont. Beyond the village the road climbs steadily through a broad valley and continues upwards through rocky outcrops to the highest point at 457 m (1500 ft). The descent runs through forestry plantation to the Nant-y-moch Reservoir and after a further short climb continues to Ponterwyd. The road climbs over 152 m (500 ft) past small lakes before a long descent to Penrhyn-coch with the countryside becoming softer, rounder and greener in the valley. There are unfortunately two stings in the tail of this ride in the form of two steep hills before the final, flat stretch into Aberystwyth.

Start

Aberystwyth Railway Station (**Or**, to avoid climb on busy A487 at start of ride, start at lay-by at instruction 2)

P Behind the back of the station (**Or** alternative starting point at lay-by at instruction 2 – junction of B4572 and A487)

Distance and grade

59 km (37 miles)

Strenuous

Terrain

Steep, grass-covered hills, forestry, reservoir, woodland. Total height gain – 1050 m (3450 ft)

Nearest railway

Aberystwyth

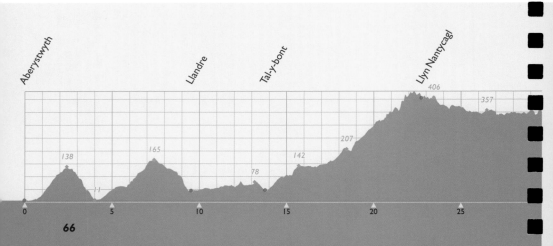

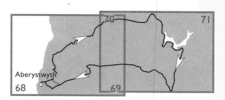

Aberystwyth
68   69   70   71

▼ *Aberystwyth*

Places of interest

Aberystwyth 1
Coastal resort and university town. Three million books are housed in the National Library of Wales where there are library treasures on show. Aberystwyth Yesterday recalls the town's past. There is also a ruined castle, a cliff railway and a camera obscura

Nant-y-Moch Reservoir 10
The dark waters of the reservoir flood the high, boggy moorlands on the slopes of the Plynlimon mountain range. The waters are held back by a buttressed stone dam, a formidable structure 52 m (172 ft) high and 351 m (1150 ft) long which traps the head-waters of the River Rheidol, forming a crescent-shaped lake 5 km (3 miles) in length. The waters are used to gener-ate energy by powering hydro-electric turbines

Refreshments
The Mill PH 🍺, plenty of choice in **Aberystwyth**
White Lion PH, Black Lion Hotel, **Tal-y-bont**
George Borrow PH, **Ponterwyd**

Ponterwyd   Llyn Blaenmelindwr   Pen-rhiw-newydd   Penrhyn-coch   Capel Dewi   Llanbadarn Fawr

391   296   294   375   431
123   114
50
5

30   35   40   45   50   55   59.3

1 With back to the railway station in Aberystwyth, go SA onto Terrace Road by the Vale of Rheidol PH 'Machynlleth, Llangurig'. Get into the LH lane. At T-j R, then stay in the middle lane following signs for 'The North, Machynlleth'

2 Unpleasant climb on busy road. After 1 km, and 270 m (300 yd) after passing beneath footbridge, next L 'Llangorwen 1½, Clarach 2½'. (This junction is the alternative starting point)

3 Descend, then climb. **Easy to miss**. 1 km after starting climb and shortly after a turning to Rhoscellan Farm to the left, take the next R, just before the gradient steepens

4 Climb. Superb views. Go past a cemetery in the woods and follow a hairpin bend round to the R. At T-j by house called Gwyndy turn L

5 At T-j with B4353 immediately after railway crossing L for 360 m (400 yd), then 2nd R onto Lon Glanfred 'Caravan Park'

6 At T-j with A487 L 'Tal-y-bont 1¼, then 1st R. Shortly, at T-j L

7 At T-j with A487 by Tal-y-bont sign R, then 1st R after the bridge by the village green 'Bontgoch (Elerch), Nant-y-moch'

8 Ignore 1st left on sharp RH bend. After 270 m (300 yd) climbing next L 'Nant-y-moch. Single track road'

➡ **page 71**

14 After 6 km (4 miles), in Penrhyn-coch, shortly after church and petrol station, turn L by Post Office and stone memorial onto a minor road just before T-j

15 Steep climb. At T-j, shortly after brow of hill, R (NS)

16 At X-roads (with A4159) SA 'Waun Fawr, Llanbadarn Fawr'

17 For return to the alternative starting point at the lay-by at instruction 2, at the brow of the hill turn R 'Waun Fawr'. For Aberystwyth railway station continue SA

18 At T-j with A44 at the bottom of steep hill R 'Aberystwyth', then immediately R again 'Aberystwyth A44'

19 At T-j with A487 (Penglas Terrace) turn L 'Cardigan' to follow one-way system back to the station

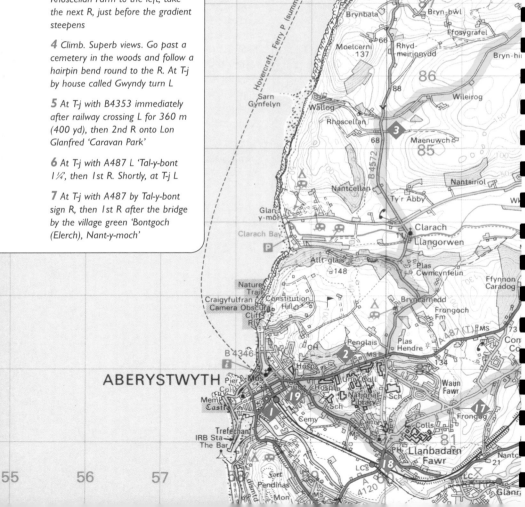

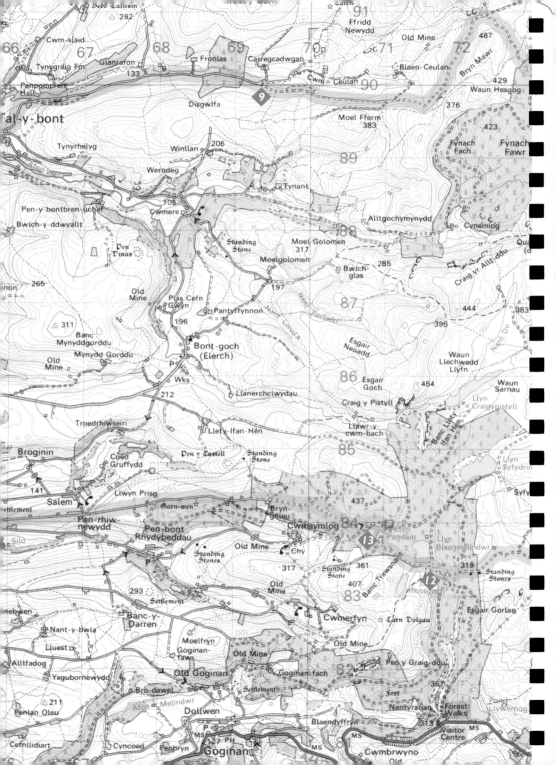

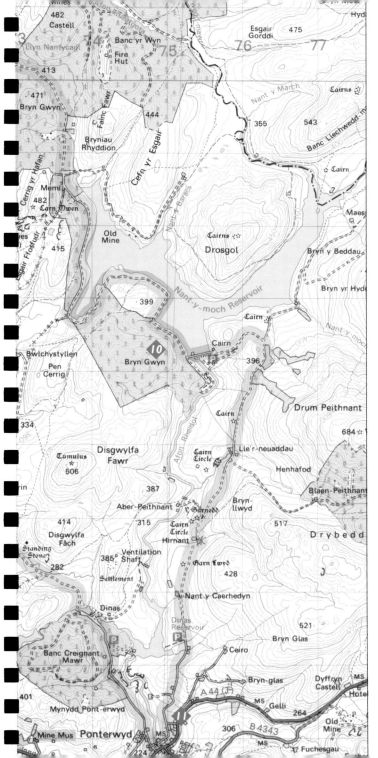

9 After 5 km (3 miles) ignore LH fork to Carregcadwgan

10 Over the next 11 km (7 miles), climb to 460 m (1500 ft), pass through forestry, descend past Nant-y-moch Reservoir

11 Climb away from Nant-y-moch Reservoir, then descend past much smaller Dinas Reservoir. On sharp LH bend, immediately after Ponterwyd sign at the start of the village, bear R (in effect SA) then shortly, 1st R over small stone bridge. At T-j R again. (For the village shop and George Borrow PH follow road to L at Ponterwyd sign)

12 Climb, then start descending. At fork 5 km (3 miles) from Ponterwyd take upper LH road 'Pendam, Penrhyncoch. Mountain road'

13 Follow signs for Aberystwyth and Penrhyncoch around the LH edge of the lake. At T-j with car parking area in the woods ahead bear L. Views of Aberystwyth and coast beyond lake

◀ page 68

Towards the source of the River Severn, west of Llanidloes

Llanidloes lies almost midway on a line across Wales at its narrowest point. For a relatively short route, this ride combines a wide variety of scenery: green fields bounded by age-old hedgerows and grazed by sheep; rich arable land; broadleaf woodland; a flat valley bottom to the east of Trefeglwys; a climb to over 396 m (1300 ft); a reservoir; forestry plantation and a delightful stretch alongside the young River Severn. The painstaking art of hedge-laying reaches its consummate expression in Mid-Wales and the Welsh Borders. They are as much a part of the region's heritage as the dry-stone walls are to the Yorkshire Dales. For those wishing to take on a tougher challenge, this ride can easily be linked to on-road Route 8 near to Staylittle.

Start

Unicorn Hotel, near Market Square, Llanidloes

P Follow signs

Distance and grade

43 km (27 miles)

Moderate

Terrain

Hills; moorland; forestry and pasture. Total height gain – 605 m (2000 ft)

Nearest railway

Caersws, 3 km (2 miles) northeast of the route at instruction 5

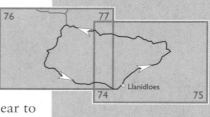

76   77

74   Llanidloes   75

▶ *Llyn Clywedog*

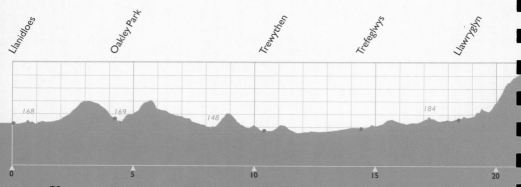

Refreshments

Plenty of choice in **Llanidloes**
Red Lion PH, **Trefeglwys**

Staylittle
Dolydd
Hafren Forest
Tan Hinon
Glan-y-nant

359
307
290
372
351
302
259
209
233
168
126
403

25
30
35
40
42.7

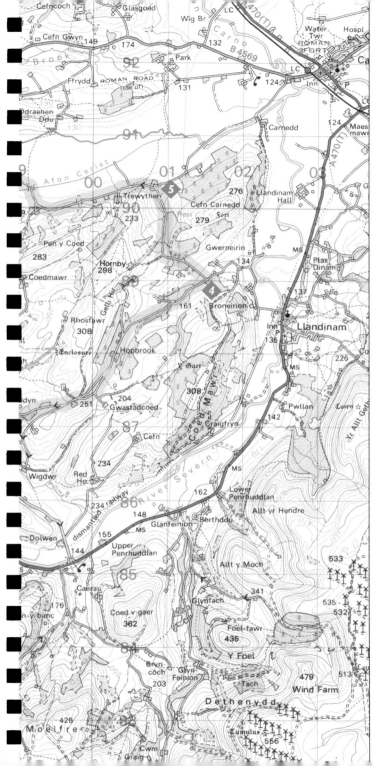

1 With your back to the Unicorn Hotel (near the Market Hall) in Llanidloes L along Long Bridge Street. At mini roundabout, L over bridge 'B4569 Llynclywedog, Trefeglwys'

2 After 800 m (½ mile), at the start of the hill, 1st proper road to the R 'Oakley Park 2'

3 **Easy to miss**. Climb up and over brow of hill. 800 m (½ mile) after the brow, ignore the 1st left on descent. Shortly, take the next L 'Llandinam 3, Caersws 5¼' – 90 m (100 yd) before the telephone box

4 Ignore two left turns (these are no through roads, not signed). On flatter section, 5 km (3 miles) after the last instruction, take next L 'Caersws 2¾, Trefeglwys 3½'

5 Climb, then descend. At T-j L 'Trefeglwys 2¾'

6 At T-j (with B4569) in Trefeglwys L then, shortly after Red Lion PH, take the next R by the Post Office and store 'Llawryglyn 2'

7 After 5 km (3 miles), shortly after passing a chapel and cemetery on the right in Llawryglyn, take the next R at the top of a short hill

➡ page 76

7 *After 5 km (3 miles), shortly after passing a chapel and cemetery on the right in Llawryglyn, take the next R at the top of a short hill*

8 *3 km (2 mile) climb with some very steep parts. Superb views. At T-j, shortly after the highest point, R downhill*

9 *Steep descent. At T-j (with B4518) R 'Llanbrynmair 7'. Ignore 1st left by telephone box, take next L 'Llwynygog ½'. (**Or** for link to on-road Route 8, at T-j with B4518 turn R for about 1 km then L immediately after bridge to join Route 8 at instruction 14)*

10 *Follow this road for 18 km (11 miles) back to the start, the last 11 km (7 miles) of which are alongside the young River Severn*

Places of interest

Llanidloes 1
The first settlement on the River Severn, Britain's longest river, which rises on the slopes of Plynlimon, 16 km (10 miles) to the west. King Edward I granted the town a market chapter in 1280. It has pleasant, tree-lined streets in the shape of a cross and in the middle is the old half-timbered Market Hall, built in about 1600 and now the only one of its kind in Wales. A museum occupies the old courtroom above

Staylittle 9
There are two suggestions for the name of the village: one is that the local blacksmiths could shoe horses so fast that impatient travellers need only 'stay a little'; the other is that the inhospitable attitude of the villagers made visitors pass through quickly. Further north, a minor road turns west off the B4518 to where the River Twymyn plunges down Ffrwyd Fawr – one of the highest waterfalls in Wales

Llyn Clywedog 10
A huge dam, the tallest in Britain at 83 m (273 ft), was built in 1968 thus solving the flooding problems of the Severn Valley and creating opportunities for water sports on the reservoir

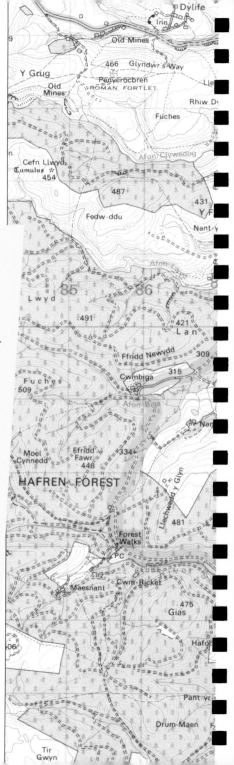

Bishop's Castle, Montgomery and the Kerry Ridgeway

Both Bishop's Castle and Montgomery lie very close to the border between England and Wales. Both are attractive towns with a fine selection of pubs and tea shops. North from the start the ride heads for the hills that are collectively known as the Shropshire Highlands. The wooded section in the valley of the West Onny is a real delight but is followed by a steep climb of almost 213 m (700 ft) in the next 2 km (1½ miles). The long, fast descent from the top is followed by a flat section of some 18 km (11 miles) right into Montgomery. The second set of hills lie between the Severn Valley to the west and the curiously named River Caebitra in the east. Beyond Sarn, and visible for many miles, is the final challenge of the day: the climb up onto Kerry Ridgeway. The first section is very steep but the 10 km (6 mile) ridge and descent beyond the high point are a fitting end to this tough ride.

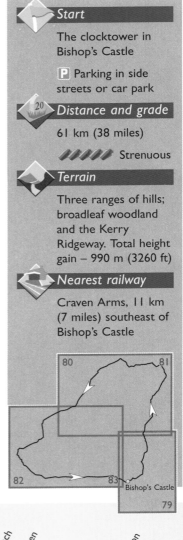

Start

The clocktower in Bishop's Castle

P Parking in side streets or car park

Distance and grade

61 km (38 miles)

///// Strenuous

Terrain

Three ranges of hills; broadleaf woodland and the Kerry Ridgeway. Total height gain – 990 m (3260 ft)

Nearest railway

Craven Arms, 11 km (7 miles) southeast of Bishop's Castle

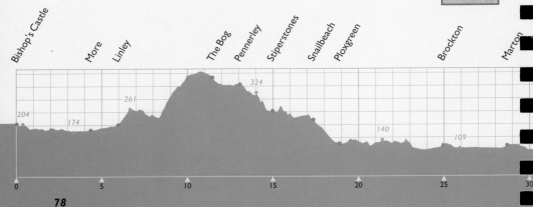

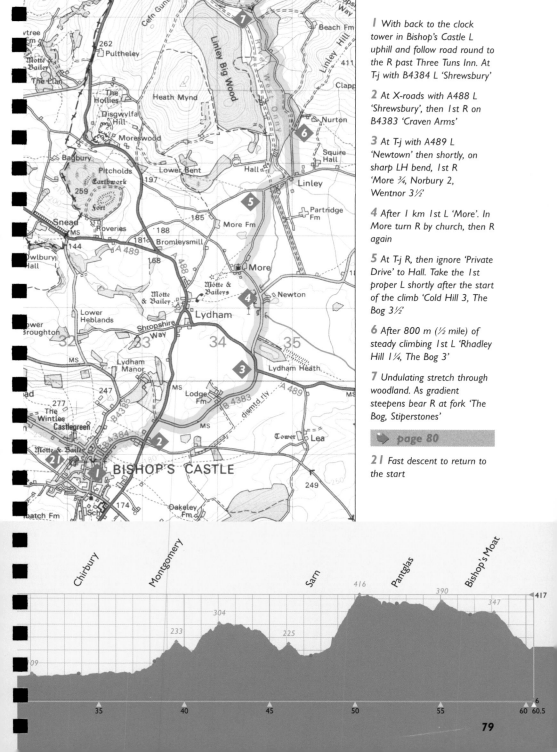

1 With back to the clock tower in Bishop's Castle L uphill and follow road round to the R past Three Tuns Inn. At T-j with B4384 L 'Shrewsbury'

2 At X-roads with A488 L 'Shrewsbury', then 1st R on B4383 'Craven Arms'

3 At T-j with A489 L 'Newtown' then shortly, on sharp LH bend, 1st R 'More ¾, Norbury 2, Wentnor 3½'

4 After 1 km 1st L 'More'. In More turn R by church, then R again

5 At T-j R, then ignore 'Private Drive' to Hall. Take the 1st proper L shortly after the start of the climb 'Cold Hill 3, The Bog 3½'

6 After 800 m (½ mile) of steady climbing 1st L 'Rhadley Hill 1¼, The Bog 3'

7 Undulating stretch through woodland. As gradient steepens bear R at fork 'The Bog, Stiperstones'

➡ page 80

21 Fast descent to return to the start

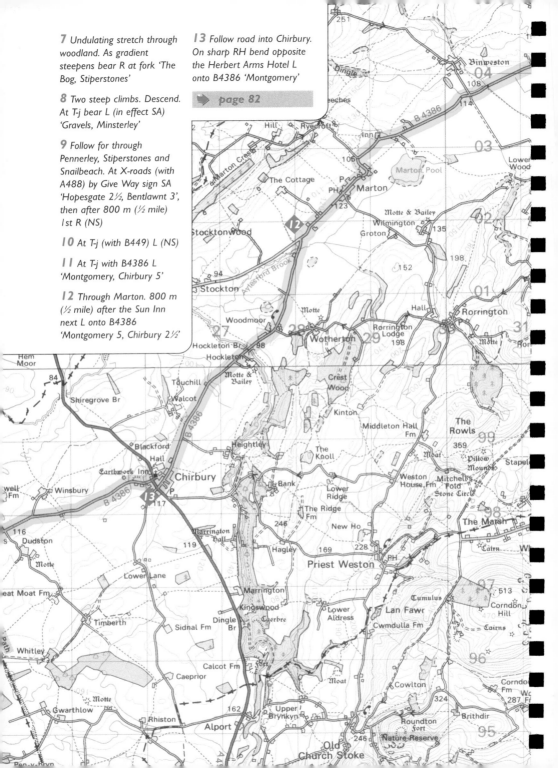

7 Undulating stretch through woodland. As gradient steepens bear R at fork 'The Bog, Stiperstones'

8 Two steep climbs. Descend. At T-j L (in effect SA) 'Gravels, Minsterley'

9 Follow for through Pennerley, Stiperstones and Snailbeach. At X-roads (with A488) by Give Way sign SA 'Hopesgate 2½, Bentlawnt 3', then after 800 m (½ mile) 1st R (NS)

10 At T-j (with B449) L (NS)

11 At T-j with B4386 L 'Montgomery, Chirbury 5'

12 Through Marton. 800 m (½ mile) after the Sun Inn next L onto B4386 'Montgomery 5, Chirbury 2½'

13 Follow road into Chirbury. On sharp RH bend opposite the Herbert Arms Hotel L onto B4386 'Montgomery'

➡ **page 82**

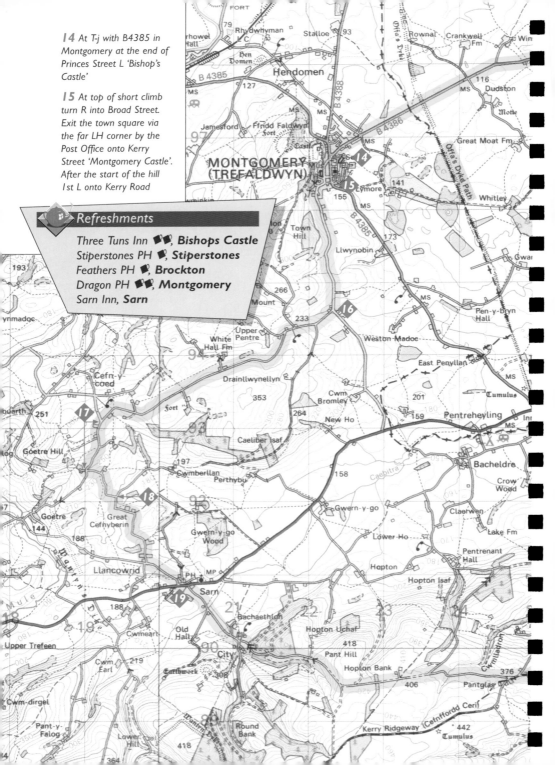

14 At T-j with B4385 in Montgomery at the end of Princes Street L 'Bishop's Castle'

15 At top of short climb turn R into Broad Street. Exit the town square via the far LH corner by the Post Office onto Kerry Street 'Montgomery Castle'. After the start of the hill 1st L onto Kerry Road

Refreshments

Three Tuns Inn, **Bishops Castle**
Stiperstones PH, **Stiperstones**
Feathers PH, **Brockton**
Dragon PH, **Montgomery**
Sarn Inn, **Sarn**

16 At the bottom of the descent 1st R 'Cefn-y-coed'

17 Steep climb. Superb views. At T-j by triangle of grass L 'Sarn 1¾, Kerry 4', then **easy to miss** after 800 m (½ mile) 1st L on fast descent

18 Ignore 'No Through Road' to the left on sharp RH bend half way down the hill. Near the bottom of the hill follow the road round to the L, ignoring a 'No through road' to the right

19 At T-j (with A489) by the Sarn Inn L, then 1st R by telephone box and bus stop

20 Climb steeply. Fine views from the ridge. After 10 km (6 miles), at T-j by triangle of grass at the junction of several roads continue SA in the same direction

21 Fast descent to return to the start

◀ page 79

Places of interest

Bishop's Castle 1
A border town set in a lush country of streams and water meadows. Little remains of the castle built by the Bishop of Hereford in 1127 but there are three Tudor houses including the House on Crutches, its overhanging upper storey supported by posts. The 17th-century Three Tuns Inn has its own brewery

Stiperstones 8
Jagged rocks mark the spine of of the heather-dark ridge in this wild country

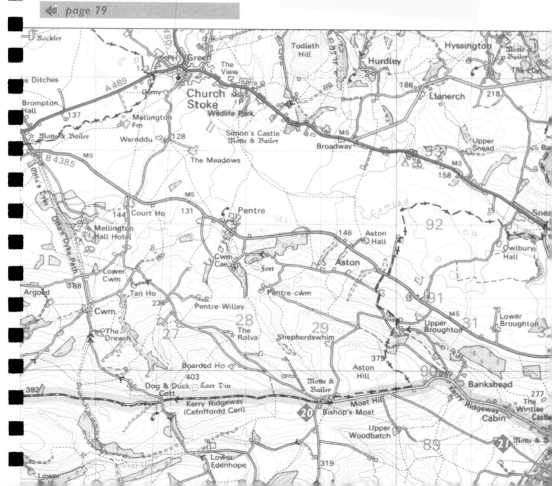

12 The Long Mynd, from Church Stretton

Start

The Railway Station, Church Stretton

P As above, or in other long stay car parks

Distance

37 km (23 miles)

Moderate

Terrain

Steep climb over heather-clad hills then farmland and woods (one steep push – the rest is easy). Total height gain – 545 m (1800 ft)

Nearest railway

Church Stretton

The shortest of the on-road rides in the book is difficult to grade: although the initial climb out of Church Stretton is at times very steep, and will probably involve pushing, once at the summit of the Long Mynd the rest of the ride is easy with little further climbing. (If you could only persuade someone to drop you at the top!) You may well wish to celebrate your crossing of this mighty range at the excellent hostelry at Bridges on the western flanks of the hillside. A well graded climb carries you north over Cothercott Hill to Pulverbatch, site of a second fine refreshment stop. This road continues northwards running gently downhill for several kilometres and would be the preferred route for a visit to Shrewsbury should you wish to extend the ride. The described route turns right off the road shortly after Pulverbatch and descends on a quiet lane through lush farmland. You pass beneath the steep hills of The Lawley and Caer Caradoc to your left before returning through All Stretton back to the start.

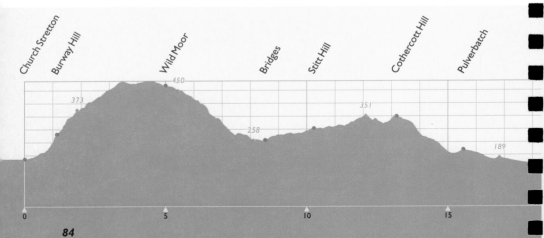

Church Stretton 1

King John granted to Church Stretton a Market Charter in 1214 and a small market is still held every Thursday in the square. Remains of the medieval town are in the High Street, once a part of the old Bristol to Chester road, an important coaching route. Promoted as a 'health resort with natural springs of pure water second to none in the country' in the early 20th century and set in 'very bracing and exhilarating surroundings'

Caer Caradoc 13/14

A hill-fort on a rocky ridge where the British chieftain Caradoc or Caractacus is said to have made his last stand against the Romans in AD 50. Castle Hill, on the other side of the valley, has a 79 m (260 ft) long mound which was possibly a Saxon fortification built over a prehistoric barrow

▲ *Lightspout Waterfall, Cardingmill Valley*

Refreshments

Plenty of choice in **Church Stretton**
Horseshoe PH 🍴🍺, **Bridges**
White Horse PH 🍴🍺, *Woodcock Inn,*
Pulverbatch
Fox Inn, **Little Ryton**
Yew Tree PH 🍺, **All Stretton**

| 88 | 89 |
| 86 | 87 |

Church Stretton

Stapleton — Little Ryton — Longnor — All Stretton

486

201

184

125

8

20   25   30   35   36.6

85

1 From the Railway Station in Church Stretton L along the main street. At X-roads with Shrewsbury Road SA onto Burway Road

2 The climb steepens after 800 m (½ mile), near the cattle grid. The next 1 km is very steep and you may well prefer to walk – enjoy the views!

3 5 km (3 miles) from Church Stretton, shortly after the first summit, 1st R 'YHA'

4 At T-j at the bottom L 'Medlicott, Bishops Castle'. Follow road round to the R signed 'Bridges'

5 At T-j R 'Pulverbatch, Shrewsbury'. Follow this road for 8 km (5 miles) on gentle climb, then gentle descent

➡ page 89

13 After 2 km (1½ miles) ignore 1st right to Leebotwood. After further 1 km next R 'Church Stretton 3¼'

14 At offset X-roads with A49 L, then R 'All Stretton ¾'

15 At T-j (with B4370) L

16 In Church Stretton, at X-roads by The Hotel L to return to the start

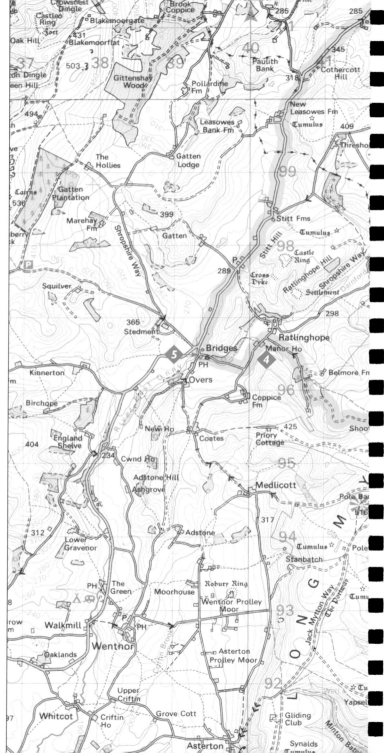

6 Through Pulverbatch, past the White Lion PH and Woodcock Inn. Descend, then climb. At the brow of the hill ignore the 1st right opposite 1874 house. Shortly, take the next R 'Moat, Stapleton'

7 At T-j L 'Stapleton, Dorrington. Follow signs for Stapleton

8 At T-j in Stapleton R 'Dorrington 1', then towards the end of the village 2nd L (NS)

9 At X-roads with the A49 SA 'Ryton ¾'

10 At X-roads SA 'Ryton ½'. At T-j by telephone box R (NS)

11 After 4 km (2½ miles), at T-j in Longnor L 'Frodesley 2¼, Acton Burnett 3½'

12 At X-roads R 'Leebotwood, Cardington, Church Stretton'

◀ **page 86**

◀ View from the Long Mynd towards Church Stretton and Wenlock Edge

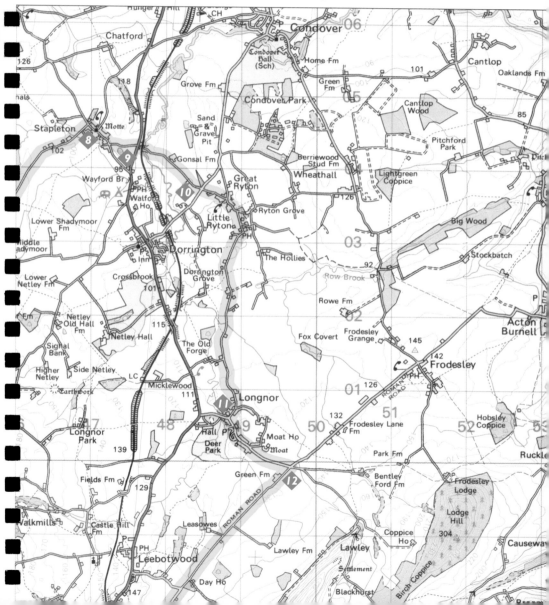

Steep Welsh Border countryside north of Knighton

13

Start
Knighton Railway Station

P As above or in the designated long stay car park near the cattle market

Distance
51 km (32 miles)

///// Strenuous

Terrain
Woodland and pasture – typical Welsh border landscape of steep hills deeply cut by streams. Total height gain – 970 m (3180 ft)

Nearest railway
Knighton

The border between England and Wales runs through Knighton and the whole area on either side of the boundary has a 'Borders' feel to it, combining the best of both countries. The Teme is the main river in the area and is followed east from Knighton to the pretty village of Bucknell where a tributary is picked up. A steep climb on one of the many tiny lanes climbs up out of the watershed of the Teme and down into that of the Clun. The village of Clun is well provided with cafes and tea shops – always popular with cyclists. The second steep climb to the highest point of the ride gives the best views of the day from the ridge that extends beyond Knuck Bank and is rewarded with a fine, 8-km (5-mile) descent back down into the Clun Valley at Newcastle. The steepest climb of the day – 198 m (650 ft) in 1.6 km (1 mile) – is the last major challenge. Savour the views at the top as the descent will require all your attention to be fixed on the road. The River Teme is joined near Llanfair Waterdine and followed back to Knighton.

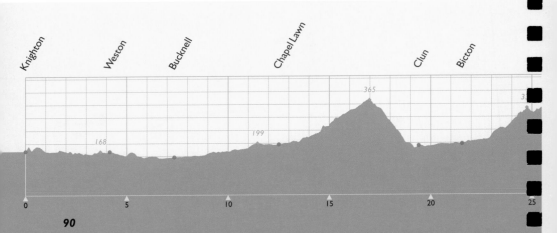

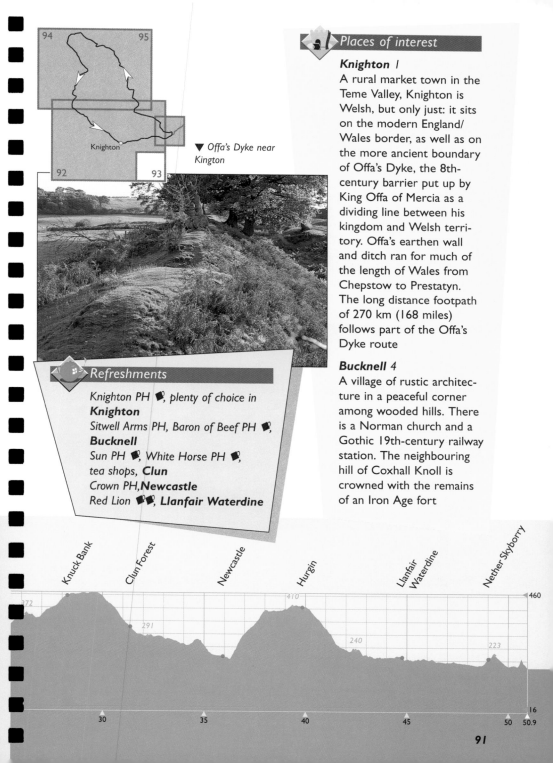

94 95

92 93

Knighton

▼ *Offa's Dyke near Kington*

Knighton 1

A rural market town in the Teme Valley, Knighton is Welsh, but only just: it sits on the modern England/ Wales border, as well as on the more ancient boundary of Offa's Dyke, the 8th-century barrier put up by King Offa of Mercia as a dividing line between his kingdom and Welsh territory. Offa's earthen wall and ditch ran for much of the length of Wales from Chepstow to Prestatyn. The long distance footpath of 270 km (168 miles) follows part of the Offa's Dyke route

Bucknell 4

A village of rustic architecture in a peaceful corner among wooded hills. There is a Norman church and a Gothic 19th-century railway station. The neighbouring hill of Coxhall Knoll is crowned with the remains of an Iron Age fort

Refreshments

Knighton PH 🍵, plenty of choice in **Knighton**
Sitwell Arms PH, Baron of Beef PH 🍺, **Bucknell**
Sun PH 🍺, White Horse PH 🍺, tea shops, **Clun**
Crown PH, **Newcastle**
Red Lion 🍺🍵, **Llanfair Waterdine**

Knuck Bank | Clun Forest | Newcastle | Hurgin | Llanfair Waterdine | Nether Skyborry

372 | 291 | 410 | 240 | 223 | 460

16

30 | 35 | 40 | 45 | 50 50.9

◄ Clun Castle

1 Out of Knighton Railway Station and turn R onto the A488 'Clun, Bishop's Castle'

2 After 1 km as the A488 swings left uphill bear R (in effect SA) 'Stone 1¼, Bucknell 3¾'

3 At X-roads SA following signs for Weston and Cubbage

4 After 5 km (3½ miles) at T-j in Bucknell at the end of Weston Road with timber yard ahead turn

L 'Clungunford 5, Craven Arms 9'. Cross railway and immediately L 'Chapel Lawn 3½ (**Or** for link to on-road Route 14 stay on B4367 to join Route 14 at instruction 14)

5 Follow for 7 km (4½ miles) passing through Chapel Lawn. Ignore left turn to 'Five Turnings' then shortly, take next R over bridge (NS)

page 94

16 At T-j L

17 Go past the Red Lion PH in Llanfair Waterdine, ignore the first left. As the road swings right towards the bridge bear L (in effect SA) 'Monaughty Poeth 1, Skyborry Green 2'

18 Follow this road for 7 km (4½ miles) through Skyborry Green (the last climb!). At T-j with A488 R to return to the start

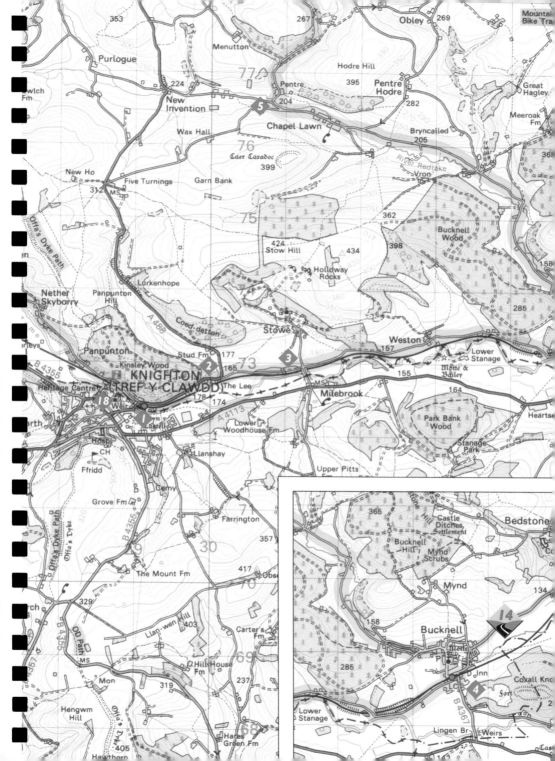

6 *After 5 km (3½ miles) at T-j with Knighton Road (A488) by triangle of grass at the bottom of hill R 'Clun'*

7 *Through Clun on A488. After 1 km 1st L 'Bicton ¾'*

8 *Ignore 1st L in Bicton. Take the 2nd L at the end of the village 'Three Gates 2¼, Mainstone 3¼'*

9 **Easy to miss.** *Cross stream, climb hill, 1st L 'Three Gates 1, Two Crosses ½'*

10 *At X-roads at Three Gates SA*

11 *At Knuck Bank X-roads at top of the hill SA. At five-way junction (Two Crosses) turn L 'Brookhouse 1½, Newcastle 4'*

12 *Follow this road downhill for 8 km (5 miles). At T-j (with B4368) in Newcastle bear L 'Clun, Craven Arms'. Cross the river and take the 1st R (NS)*

13 *Climb steeply. At X-roads at the top of the hill SA 'Cwm Collo 2, Llanfair Waterdine 3½'*

14 *At T-j L. Ignore left turn*

15 *At T-j R 'Cwm Brain ¼'. After short climb 1st L*

16 *At T-j L*

← page 92

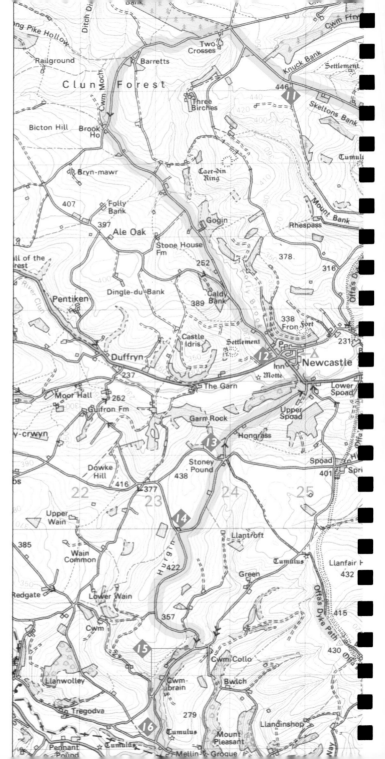

Tributaries of the River Teme, west of Ludlow

Ludlow is at or near the confluence of three rivers: the Teme, the Onny and the Corve which eventually drain into the Severn, south of Worcester. After negotiating the one-way system of Ludlow it is the course of the River Corve which is followed northwest through Stanton Lacy then up out of Corvedale and down into the Onny Valley. Craven Arms has little to delay you on your onward trip; shortly to the west you join an old Roman road that used to link Hereford with Chester. Clungunford is one of the four Shropshire villages that were linked together in the poetry of AE Housman: 'Clunton and Clunbury, Clungunford and Clun, are the quietest places under the sun'. After the ruins of Hopton Castle and the attractive villages of Bucknell and Leintwardine, there is a delightful stretch alongside the River Teme. Unfortunately the toughest climb of the day is near the end, from the Teme Valley near Burrington up through woodland before the final, exhilarating 4-km (2½-mile) descent back down into Ludlow.

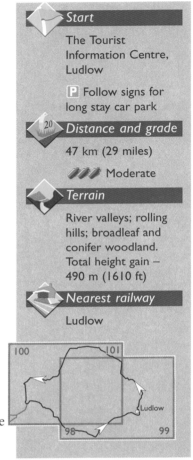

Start

The Tourist Information Centre, Ludlow

P Follow signs for long stay car park

Distance and grade

47 km (29 miles)

/// Moderate

Terrain

River valleys; rolling hills; broadleaf and conifer woodland. Total height gain – 490 m (1610 ft)

Nearest railway

Ludlow

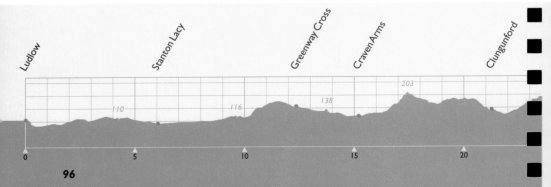

Ludlow 1

One of Britain's loveliest towns, a harmonious mix of medieval, Tudor, Stuart and Georgian buildings. Dominating all is the 11th-century castle built by a Norman knight named Roger de Lacy. The town's jumble of architectural styles is overlooked by the 41 m (135 ft) tower of St Laurence's Church. Dating from the 15th century it is one of the largest parish churches in Englandwhere the poet, AE Housman (1859–1936) is buried. Near the Butter Cross, in the Bull Ring, is the Feathers Hotel, one of the finest timber-framed buildings in England

Stokesay Castle

over 1 km south of instruction 8
A fortified manor house whose timbered additions give a cosy rather than a defensive air. Almost unchanged after 750 years. The nearby church is 17th century with texts painted on the walls

---

Refreshments

Church PH 🍴🍴, Unicorn PH 🍴🍴, *plenty of choice in* **Ludlow**
Craven Arms Hotel, **Craven Arms**
Sun PH 🍴, **Leintwardine**

▼ Ludlow

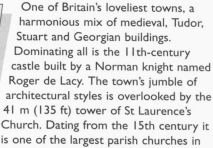

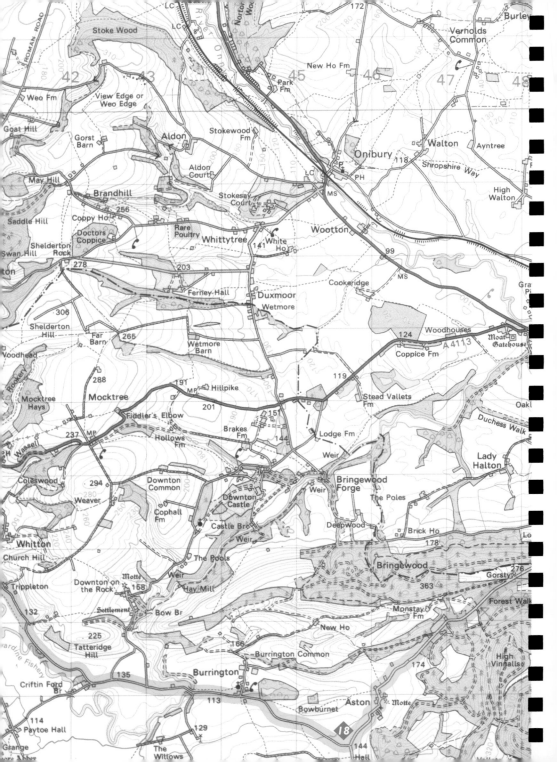

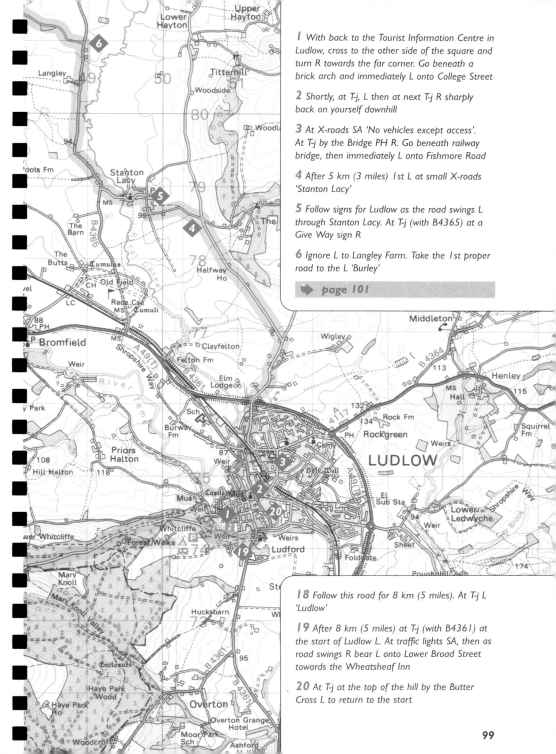

1 With back to the Tourist Information Centre in Ludlow, cross to the other side of the square and turn R towards the far corner. Go beneath a brick arch and immediately L onto College Street

2 Shortly, at T-j, L then at next T-j R sharply back on yourself downhill

3 At X-roads SA 'No vehicles except access'. At T-j by the Bridge PH R. Go beneath railway bridge, then immediately L onto Fishmore Road

4 After 5 km (3 miles) 1st L at small X-roads 'Stanton Lacy'

5 Follow signs for Ludlow as the road swings L through Stanton Lacy. At T-j (with B4365) at a Give Way sign R

6 Ignore L to Langley Farm. Take the 1st proper road to the L 'Burley'

➡ page 101

18 Follow this road for 8 km (5 miles). At T-j L 'Ludlow'

19 After 8 km (5 miles) at T-j (with B4361) at the start of Ludlow L. At traffic lights SA, then as road swings R bear L onto Lower Broad Street towards the Wheatsheaf Inn

20 At T-j at the top of the hill by the Butter Cross L to return to the start

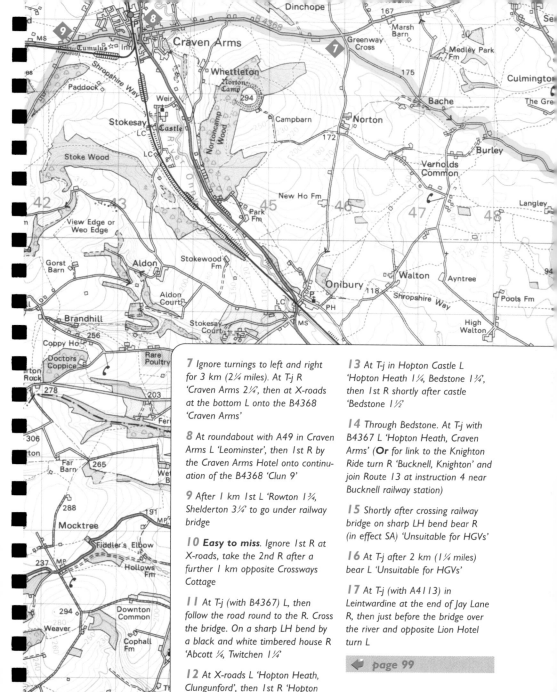

7 Ignore turnings to left and right for 3 km (2¼ miles). At T-j R 'Craven Arms 2¼', then at X-roads at the bottom L onto the B4368 'Craven Arms'

8 At roundabout with A49 in Craven Arms L 'Leominster', then 1st R by the Craven Arms Hotel onto continuation of the B4368 'Clun 9'

9 After 1 km 1st L 'Rowton 1¾, Shelderton 3¼' to go under railway bridge

10 **Easy to miss**. Ignore 1st R at X-roads, take the 2nd R after a further 1 km opposite Crossways Cottage

11 At T-j (with B4367) L, then follow the road round to the R. Cross the bridge. On a sharp LH bend by a black and white timbered house R 'Abcott ¼, Twitchen 1¼'

12 At X-roads L 'Hopton Heath, Clungunford', then 1st R 'Hopton Castle'

13 At T-j in Hopton Castle L 'Hopton Heath 1¼, Bedstone 1¾', then 1st R shortly after castle 'Bedstone 1½'

14 Through Bedstone. At T-j with B4367 L 'Hopton Heath, Craven Arms' (**Or** for link to the Knighton Ride turn R 'Bucknell, Knighton' and join Route 13 at instruction 4 near Bucknell railway station)

15 Shortly after crossing railway bridge on sharp LH bend bear R (in effect SA) 'Unsuitable for HGVs'

16 At T-j after 2 km (1¼ miles) bear L 'Unsuitable for HGVs'

17 At T-j (with A4113) in Leintwardine at the end of Jay Lane R, then just before the bridge over the river and opposite Lion Hotel turn L

◀ page 99

Into hills above the coast to the west of Conwy

The A55 runs along the coast from Chester to Bangor on a spectacular course through tunnels cut into the rocks close to the sea. Rising almost vertically from the coastline are the hills explored on this ride – this is not for the faint-hearted. Both the steep climb to Sychnant Pass at the start of the route and the fine views from the top are just a taster of what is to come. The road drops from the start to Penmaenmawr, the last chance of refreshments before the two tough, 305-m (1000-ft) climbs at the heart of the ride. The first climb starts on a steep tarmac lane which turns to track at it passes between the peaks of Foel Lûs and Craig Hafodwen. Signs point you on to the Druids' Stone Circle where you will get the most amazing views of the whole ride. Following the North Wales Path, the descent brings you down into the valley formed by Afon Ddu. The second, steeper climb back into the mountains will involve some pushing but the surface is on a good stone track. The track continues to the high point at Bwlch y Ddeufaen before a long, fast descent to Rowen, refreshments and undulating lanes back to the start.

Start

The car park at the base of Sychnant Pass 2 km (1½ miles) to the west of Conwy (GR 759769)

P As above

Distance and grade

29 km (18 miles)

Strenuous

Terrain

Steep climbs on good stone tracks over open mountainside. Fine sea views. Total height gain – 930 m (3050 ft)

Nearest railway

Conwy

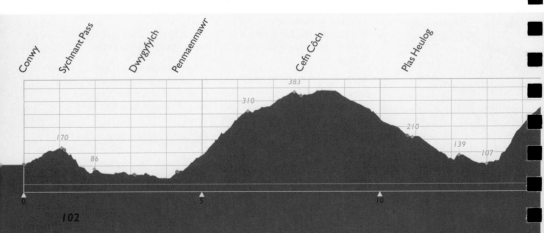

Penmaenmawr 2
William Gladstone often visited this Victorian coastal resort, squeezed between the mountains and the sea. A historic trail leads to the hill-top site of Stone Age flint works 366 m (1200 ft) above the town. There are views across to Puffin Island where puffins breed

Rowen 13
Romans came here in the 1st century AD and drove roads across hills and moors. West of the village the Roman road climbs to 427 m (1400 ft) and crosses mountains and moorland scattered with ancient burial chambers and standing stones

Refreshments
Plenty of choice in
Conwy
Y Dwygyflchi PH, Fairy Glen PH, tea shop,
Dwygyflchi
Plenty of choice in
Penmaenmawr
Willow Tea Garden, Ty Gwyn Hotel, **Rowen**
Tea room at Conwy Valley Fisheries (near instruction 14)

◄ Near Bethesda, Carnedds

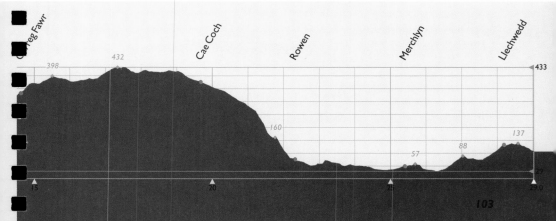

1 From the car park to the west of Conwy at the base of Sychnant Pass, turn L uphill towards and over the Sychnant Pass

2 Through Dwygyfylchi. At the start of Penmaenmawr 1st L on Graiglwyd Road by the Catholic Church of Our Lady of the Rosary

3 After 800 m (½ mile) 1st L onto Mountain Lane 'Green Gorge, Jubilee Palm, Old Church, Druids Circle'

4 Follow this lane steeply uphill. Tarmac turns to track and swings sharp R uphill on hairpin bend near two round stone pillars

5 Keep bearing R through red and white 'No Entry' signs (no vehicles) and following signs for 'Druids Circle'. After the final house the track becomes rougher and soon swings sharp R uphill through gate, then L 'North Wales Path'

6 Go past immaculately pointed stone hut and beneath power lines. Pass to the R of and beneath the Druids Circle which lies up to your left. At fork of tracks soon after the Druids Circle bear L on the upper track

7 The track turns to tarmac soon after the farm. At T-j L

8 At T-j, shortly after a RH hairpin bend by the stream, turn L over the bridge, then at next T-j R to rejoin North Wales Path

9 **Easy to miss**. Shortly, after passing golf course on the right, and at the top of a hill just before the road swings right downhill, turn L through gate by a stone farm and barns all in a row 'No cars or motorbikes'

10 Long, steep climb with wonderful views opening up behind. The North Wales Path joins from the left. Shortly, fork L following 'North Wales Path' sign

11 At fork by the pylons bear L, then at X-roads L again on slightly downhill track, following the line of pylons

12 After 3 km (2 miles) track turns to tarmac. After over 1 km of tarmac 1st track/lane to the L

13 Track turns back to tarmac near the Youth Hostel. Very steep road descent. At T-j in Rowen turn L and follow road past the Post Office

14 After 1 km, and 400 m (¼ mile) after Conwy Valley Fisheries, next lane L 'Henryd'

15 At T-j at the bottom of short steep hill R 'Henryd', then 1st L (NS)

16 At T-j R 'Groesffordd ½, Conwy 2', then after 800 m (½ mile) 1st L 'Sychnant' to return to the start

Take care not to mistake the faded yellow line of the national park boundary for the solid yellow line of the route

2 *Mountain tracks and a Roman road near Betws-y-Coed*

Betws-y-Coed is the real tourist centre of Snowdonia but you soon escape on a quiet lane, parallel with the Afon Llugwy, and disappear into forestry. The river valley is followed westwards on a second minor lane and before long you are up into the hills on a steep, stony track which will require 800 m (½ mile) of pushing to reach the cross-roads of tracks near to the quarry. The track improves in the forestry and a fast descent brings you down to Dolwyddelan and a chance for refreshment. There follows a delightful valley section between stone walls, through pasture and woodland, parallel to the railway. A second hill must be climbed and the course of the old Roman road of Sarn Helen is followed steeply northeast then down towards Betws-y-Coed. The last downhill section is fairly technical and care should be taken, particularly in wet conditions.

NB It is easy to link this ride with off-road Route 3. The best sequence would be to leave Route 3 at instruction 7, join this route at instruction 4, follow until instruction 15 then join the waymarked, southern forestry route back to Betws-y-Coed.

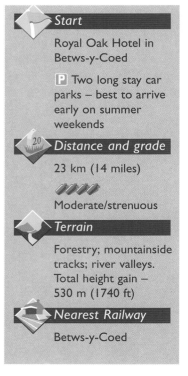

Start
Royal Oak Hotel in Betws-y-Coed

P Two long stay car parks – best to arrive early on summer weekends

Distance and grade
23 km (14 miles)

Moderate/strenuous

Terrain
Forestry; mountainside tracks; river valleys. Total height gain – 530 m (1740 ft)

Nearest Railway
Betws-y-Coed

▶ *Llyn Mymbyr and Snowdon at dusk*

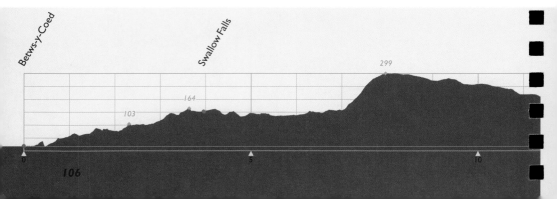

Betws-y-Coed 1

A busy tourist village with wall-to-wall accommodation establishments, set among conifer-clad crags above the confluence of Conwy and Llugwy rivers. There are historic bridges, waterfalls, beauty spots, salmon leaps and walks and the National Park Visitor Centre

Sarn Helen 12-17

The main Roman road along the western side of Wales ran from Camarthen via Aberystwyth and Dolgellau to the Conwy Valley. Much of it is over difficult country and parts of it have not yet been identified with certainty. It is followed during this ride between the A470 and the A5

Refreshments

Plenty of choice in **Betws-y-Coed**
Castle Elen Hotel, Y Gwydyr PH,
Dolwyddelan

Dolwyddelan

Pont-y-pant

262
300
163
148
133
50
133
15
20
17
22.8

1 With back to the Royal Oak Hotel in Betws-y-Coed turn L, then 1st R over river on the B5106 'Trefriw'. 1st L immediately after bridge 'Parking, Toilets'

2 **Easy to miss**. After 3 km (2 miles), shortly after passing white stone cottage on the right and crossing small bridge over stream, **ignore** 1st left, turn towards houses, start climbing steeply and take the next L by wooden barrier onto forestry track

3 Ignore the 1st downhill track to the left (yellow markers). At fork of tracks take the next L on the lower of the two tracks

4 At T-j with road L downhill (**Or** R downhill from off-road Route 3). At T-j (with A5) L over bridge, then immediately R

5 Ignore left to Bryn Gefeilia. Take the next track to the L towards a large stone house 'Public footpath'

6 Steep stony push. At fork bear L on steeper, stony track

7 At offset X-roads of tracks near to the top of climb L, then R ('Quarry' is signed to the right)

8 The brow is reached soon after the quarry X-roads. Shortly, after passing a small stone hut near a gate at the start of the forestry, ignore three right turns and follow the good forestry track down to the road

9 At T-j (with A470) turn R. **Busy road. Take care**. After 1 km, opposite the Y Gwydyr PH turn L 'Dolwyddelan railway station'

10 Cross bridge over River Lledr, then immediately L 'Parking, Railway station'

11 Follow lane past school and playing fields. Tarmac turns to track. Go through several gates, past Pont-y-pant Railway Station and bear L by Plas Hotel over bridge

12 At T-j with A470 turn L, then 1st lane R

13 At X-roads by Fron Goch SA onto broad, stone track

14 Track becomes rougher and enters forest. At offset X-roads with broader forestry track L, then R

15 At X-roads with forestry track soon after house on the left (there is a green and white bike sign to the right) continue SA downhill through gates on narrow track (blue marker). (**Or** for longer route, turn R at X-roads with forestry track and follow the waymarked forestry bike route back to Betws-y-Coed)

16 Steep stony descent. At X-roads near house on right SA downhill

17 At T-j with A5 R downhill to return to the start

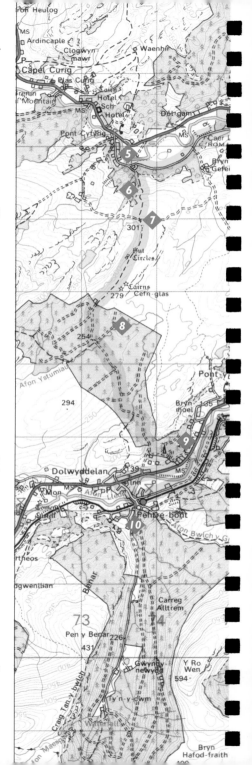

3 *Two waymarked routes in Gwydir Forest Park, Betws-y-Coed*

With the exception of parts of Scotland there are more Forestry Commission holdings with good off-road cycling opportunities in Mid- and North Wales than in any other part of Britain. Many of these have been waymarked and offer all-year-round riding. The Gwydir Forest Park, centred on Betws-y-Coed, has two waymarked loops of 18 and 11 km (11 and 7 miles) which can be linked to the off-road Route 2 from Betws-y-Coed to form a tough challenge. Both rides are best undertaken anti-clockwise for the clearest waymarking. Both offer a mixture of fine mountain and lake views, mainly rideable climbs and fast descents.

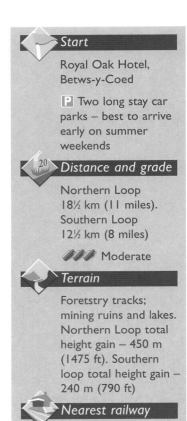

Start

Royal Oak Hotel, Betws-y-Coed

P Two long stay car parks – best to arrive early on summer weekends

Distance and grade

Northern Loop
18½ km (11 miles).
Southern Loop
12½ km (8 miles)

Moderate

Terrain

Foretstry tracks; mining ruins and lakes. Northern Loop total height gain – 450 m (1475 ft). Southern loop total height gain – 240 m (790 ft)

Nearest railway

Betws-y-Coed

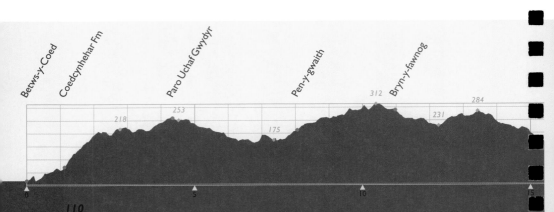

Other Forestry Commission holdings in this area

◆ Newborough Forest in the southwest corner of Anglesey

◆ Beddgelert (bike hire at 01766 890434). On A4085 southeast of Caernarfon

◆ Clocaenog (waymarked bike route starts from GR 064556) and Mynydd Hiraethog. Near Llyn Brenig and Alwen Reservoirs, west of Ruthin

◆ Coed y Brenin (bike hire at 01766 87569). Four trails, all starting from the Visitor Centre, GR715276, off the A470, 14 km (9 miles) north of Dolgellau

Fun Route, 11 km (7 miles), Yellow Sport Route, 24 km (14 miles), Blue Expert Route, 37 km (23 miles), Red Race route, 11 km (7 miles), Red Bull

◆ Penllyn Forest and several other forestry holdings south of Bala

◆ Dyfi Forest, north of Machynlleth, several other forestry holdings south of Machynlleth

◆ Dyfnant Forest and several other forestry holdings south and east of Lake Vyrnwy (See off-road Route 9)

◆ Rheidol Forest/Nant yr Arian. West of Ponterwyd on the A44. Please avoid using the waymarked footpaths to the north of the Nant-yr-Arian Visitor Centre

◆ Hafren Forest and several other forestry holdings between Llangurig and Devil's Bridge either side of the A44 (see off-road Route 10)

◆ Coed Sarnau Forest, north of Llandrindod Wells

◆ Hopton Titterhill waymarked route northeast of Knighton. Several short woodland routes in the triangle formed by Ludlow, Bishop's Castle and Kington: Colstey Woods and Bury Ditches; Wapley Hill; Shobdon Hill Wood; Mere Hill Wood; Mortimer Forest

Refreshments

Plenty of choice in **Betws-y-Coed**

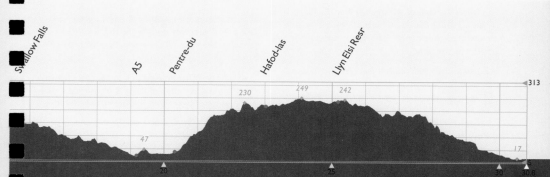

▼ Swallow Falls

Southern loop

I With back to the Royal Oak Hotel in Betws-y-Coed turn L on the A5 towards Bangor for just over I km

A Soon after passing the Miners Bridge Arms PH take next lane L 'Unsuitable for motors', then immediately R steeply uphill (bike sign). Bear R uphill by Garth Falls signpost. Follow bike signs. This will shortly involve one steep, stony climb where you will have to push. Follow bike signs on easier tracks past Llyn Elsi. At T-j with lane L, then at T-j (with A5) L to return to start

I With back to the Royal Oak Hotel in Betws-y-Coed turn L, then after 800 m (½ mile) 1st R over river on the B5106 'Trefriw', then immediately L after bridge 'Parking, Toilets'

2 Ignore 1st right on No through road. Continue climbing. After 800 m (½ mile) shortly, after dip to cross small stream, next R uphill on steep tarmac lane by green bike sign

3 Steep road climb. 400 m (¼ mile) after passing Penrallt Ganol Farm on sharp LH bend next track R (bike sign). Follow bike signs through several junctions. Go past lake (Llyn y Paro) and climb to brow of hill. On descent, bear R at two junctions (bike signs). **Easy to miss.** As downhill gradient steepens keep an eye out for a L turn sharply back on yourself

4 Keep following bike signs. At T-j with road L, then R past the mining ruins

5 Follow bike route signs in a loop to the north, then south past Llyn Glangors. At T-j with road R

6 Soon after passing road on the right signed 'Llyn Geirionydd' take next track to the R and keep following bike signs. (There is one **easy to miss** right turn!)

7 At road SA (**Or** turn R for link to the other Betws-y-Coed Route – join off-road Route 2 at instruction 4) At T-j (with A5) L over bridge, then immediately R

8 Fast descent. At T-j with 2nd road R downhill to return to Betws-y-Coed

4 The heart of the Clwyd Hills, west from Nannerch

The Clwyd Hills, bounded by the A541 to the north and the B5429 to the west have a fine network of bridleways, byways and unclassified roads and, along the western escarpment, some of the finest views in the country from one of its most excellent tracks. From Nannerch the route climbs towards, then parallel to, the ridge of the hills along a mixture of quiet country lanes and broad stone tracks. The major climb takes you up to a cross-roads where the views on a fine day are jaw-dropping. The magnificent track which contours south-wards along the escarpment is surely one of the best in the country. The continuation of the track beyond the road is now gently uphill and will be hard going in winter. At the second road you have the option of a short cut back to Nannerch or of adding a second loop with a tough climb on a broad, stony track followed by a long descent the other side. Both routes link for a bone-shaking descent down to the A541 and the return to the start.

 Start

Cross Foxes PH, Nannerch, 11 km (7 miles) west of Mold on the A541

 P No specific car park – between the pub and the church the road is at its widest. Please show consideration

 Distance and grade

29 km (18 miles). (20 km (12 miles) on the short route)

///// Strenuous (or moderate for the short route)

 Terrain

Tracks over the Clwyd Hills with magnificent views. Total height gain – 720 m (2365 ft), or 430 m (1410 ft) on the short route

Nearest railway

Flint, 10 km (6 miles) northeast of Nannerch

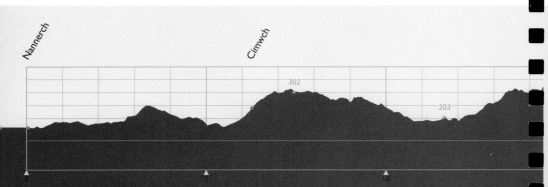

Jubilee Tower, Moel Famau *south of the route at 15*

The tower was built in 1820 to commemorate the diamond jubilee of George III (1760-1820). The original tower was blown down shortly after being built. The massive base still remains and is used as a viewing platform, with sighting plaques set in the walls

Offa's Dyke Path *15*

Opened in 1971, this long distance path runs 270 km (168 miles) from the coast near Prestatyn to the Severn Estuary. About 96 km (60 miles) of this route follows the ancient earthwork, known as Offa's Dyke. This earthwork – consisting of a ditch to the west and a ridge up to 6 m (20 ft) high behind it – was built to mark the boundary, agreed in the late 8th century, between the Celtic princes of Wales and Offa, the Saxon king of Mercia. The dyke was built piecemeal, under the aegis of local rulers, and is therefore rather patchy. There was an apparent lack of enthusiasm for the project locally: the dyke should have run to the east of the Clwydian Hills, but this section was never completed

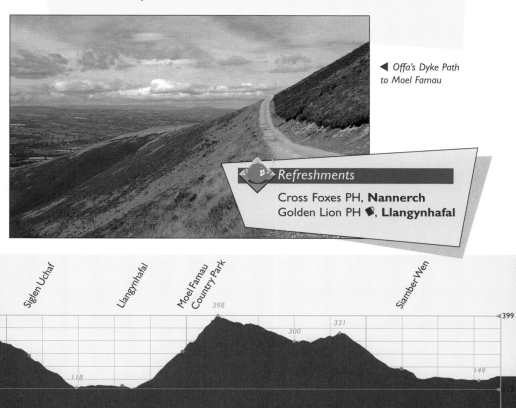

◀ *Offa's Dyke Path to Moel Famau*

Refreshments

Cross Foxes PH, **Nannerch**
Golden Lion PH 🍺, **Llangynhafal**

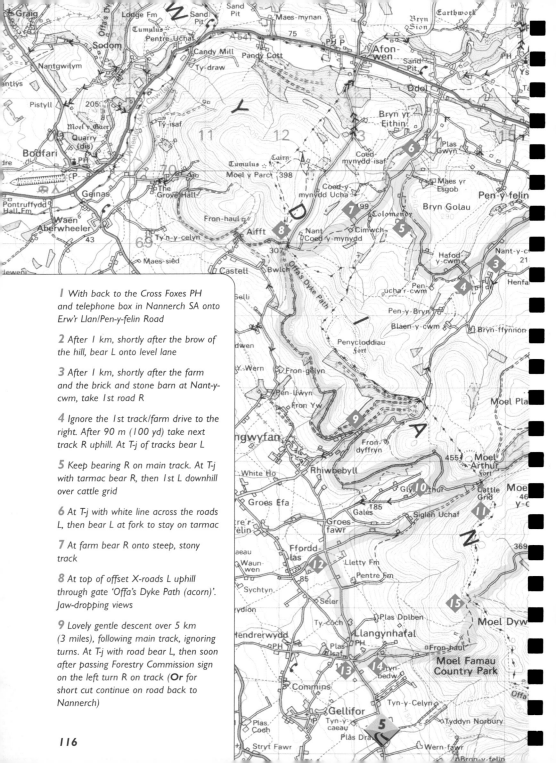

1 With back to the Cross Foxes PH and telephone box in Nannerch SA onto Erw'r Llan/Pen-y-felin Road

2 After 1 km, shortly after the brow of the hill, bear L onto level lane

3 After 1 km, shortly after the farm and the brick and stone barn at Nant-y-cwm, take 1st road R

4 Ignore the 1st track/farm drive to the right. After 90 m (100 yd) take next track R uphill. At T-j of tracks bear L

5 Keep bearing R on main track. At T-j with tarmac bear R, then 1st L downhill over cattle grid

6 At T-j with white line across the roads L, then bear L at fork to stay on tarmac

7 At farm bear R onto steep, stony track

8 At top of offset X-roads L uphill through gate 'Offa's Dyke Path (acorn)'. Jaw-dropping views

9 Lovely gentle descent over 5 km (3 miles), following main track, ignoring turns. At T-j with road bear L, then soon after passing Forestry Commission sign on the left turn R on track (**Or** for short cut continue on road back to Nannerch)

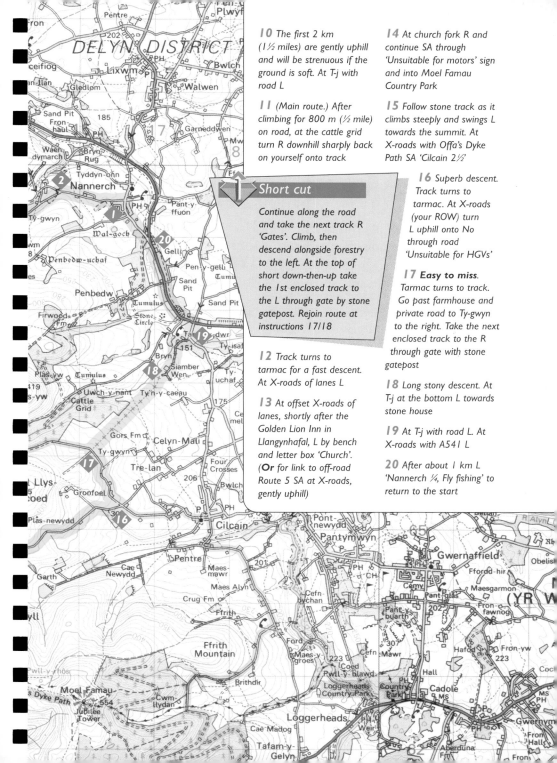

10 The first 2 km (1½ miles) are gently uphill and will be strenuous if the ground is soft. At T-j with road L

11 (Main route.) After climbing for 800 m (½ mile) on road, at the cattle grid turn R downhill sharply back on yourself onto track

12 Track turns to tarmac for a fast descent. At X-roads of lanes L

13 At offset X-roads of lanes, shortly after the Golden Lion Inn in Llangynhafal, L by bench and letter box 'Church'. (**Or** for link to off-road Route 5 SA at X-roads, gently uphill)

14 At church fork R and continue SA through 'Unsuitable for motors' sign and into Moel Famau Country Park

15 Follow stone track as it climbs steeply and swings L towards the summit. At X-roads with Offa's Dyke Path SA 'Cilcain 2½'

16 Superb descent. Track turns to tarmac. At X-roads (your ROW) turn L uphill onto No through road 'Unsuitable for HGVs'

17 **Easy to miss.** Tarmac turns to track. Go past farmhouse and private road to Ty-gwyn to the right. Take the next enclosed track to the R through gate with stone gatepost

18 Long stony descent. At T-j at the bottom L towards stone house

19 At T-j with road L. At X-roads with A541 L

20 After about 1 km L 'Nannerch ¼, Fly fishing' to return to the start

Short cut

Continue along the road and take the next track R 'Gates'. Climb, then descend alongside forestry to the left. At the top of short down-then-up take the 1st enclosed track to the L through gate by stone gatepost. Rejoin route at instructions 17/18

5 East from Ruthin into the southern Clwyd Hills

Ruthin is a charming small town with a large hill-top square surrounded by attractive old buildings and inns. Heading east from here the Clwyd Hills loom in front of you. The tarmac lane turns to track and starts climbing steeply through broadleaf woodland and becomes somewhat rougher, beyond the A494, as it climbs to the first of the two 400 m (1300 ft) high points. There are fabulous views to the east across the valley of the River Alyn. A long descent to the road is followed by a climb through forestry where an abundance of signs makes it clear where you may not cycle! Tracks and lanes lead you to the excellent hostelry at Cilcain, from where the third major climb of the day takes you up on a lane then a broad stony track to a cross-roads with Offa's Dyke Path. Should you feel in need of a longer challenge, it is easy to link this ride with off-road route 4 at the cross-roads to the west of Cilcain. From the panoramic views at the second high point there is a long, fast, open descent on a broad stony track down to the network of lanes that will take you back to Ruthin.

Start

The main square in the centre of Ruthin

P Follow signs for long stay car park

Distance and grade

30 km (19 miles)

Strenuous

Terrain

Open hill tracks and forestry tracks through the Clwyd Hills. Total height gain – 650 m (2130 ft)

Nearest railway

Little Mountain (between Buckley and Wrexham), 13 km (8 miles) east of the route near Moel Famau Forest

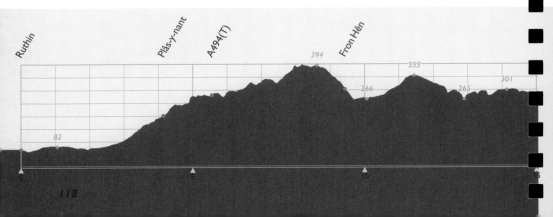

▼ *Cilcain church*

Refreshments

Plenty of choice in **Ruthin**
Clwyd Gate Inn, on A494 at instruction 6
White Horse Inn 🍴🍺, **Cilcain**

Places of interest

Forestry Commission
During the course of this ride the patchwork of different conifers used by the Forestry Commission can be very clearly seen. Larches, brown and leafless in winter, but light green in summer, contrast with the darker green of of Douglas firs and the bluey-green of spruce. Each species is chosen for particular conditions. Douglas firs grow well on steep, rocky hillsides and can tolerate shade. The Sitka spruce survives damp conditions and will grow up to altitudes of 430 m (1400 ft)

Llanarmon-yn-Ial *3 km (2 miles) east of the route* A peaceful village in the valley of the River Alyn. Limestone cottages and a whitewashed inn cluster around the double-naved medieval church which contains an effigy of the 14th-century hero Llywelyn ap Gruffydd

Cilcain · Llangynhafal · Hirwaen

216 · 188 · 397 · 79 · 400

20 · 25 · 30

1 Leave Ruthin's main square via Well Street/Stryd-y-Ffymon 'Wrexham, Hospital'

2 At T-j bear R (in effect SA) 'Hospital', then 2nd L immediately after Olde Anchor Inn 'Hospital'

3 Follow through red sandstone cutting. At T-j with B5429 at the end of St Meugans R, then L onto narrow lane

4 Go past Llanbadarn Farm. Ignore concrete track to the right. On sharp LH bend by Plas-y-plant Lodge leave tarmac and continue SA onto broad stone track

5 At fork of tracks in the woods (by Plas-y-nant) bear L to continue uphill. Shortly, at stone barns, follow track as it swings sharply L uphill

6 At T-j (with A494) by the Clwyd Gate Inn R then, shortly after the brow, 1st track L 'Bridleway, Offa's Dyke Path (acorn)'

7 Climb hill following blue arrows and Offa's Dyke waymarks, eventually forking L onto grassier, steeper track (blue arrow, acorn)

8 Short rough section. Shortly after brow leave Offa's Dyke Path and

continue SA through gate (blue arrow). Down then up towards farm. Through bri- dlegate and follow better track round to the R keeping the farm on your right

9 Through several gates on good track with fabulous views to the right. With forestry plantation ahead follow the track downhill and round to the R 'Footpath' on stone marker

10 At road L. At T-j by Give Way sign L, then after 400 m (¼ mile) 1st R by Moel Famau Forestry Commission sign. Take the RH of the two uphill forestry tracks (bike sign)

11 'No cycling' signs tell you where you can't go! At the top of climb fork R gently downhill, then shortly fork R again

12 At T-j at the bottom of fine descent R ('No cycling' sign to the left)

13 At the end of the broad forestry track at the corner of the forest turn R to cross stile towards gate and track

14 Track turns to tarmac. At T-j L ('Loggerheads' signed to the right)

15 At fork of lanes by stone cottage bear R downhill

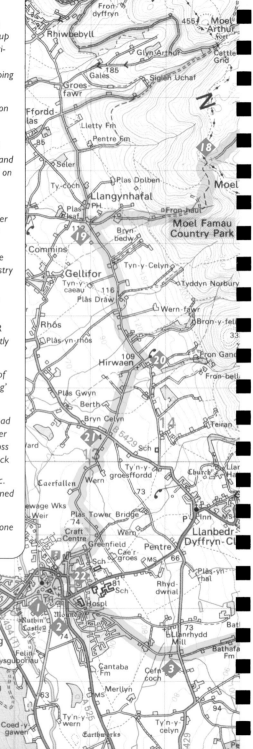

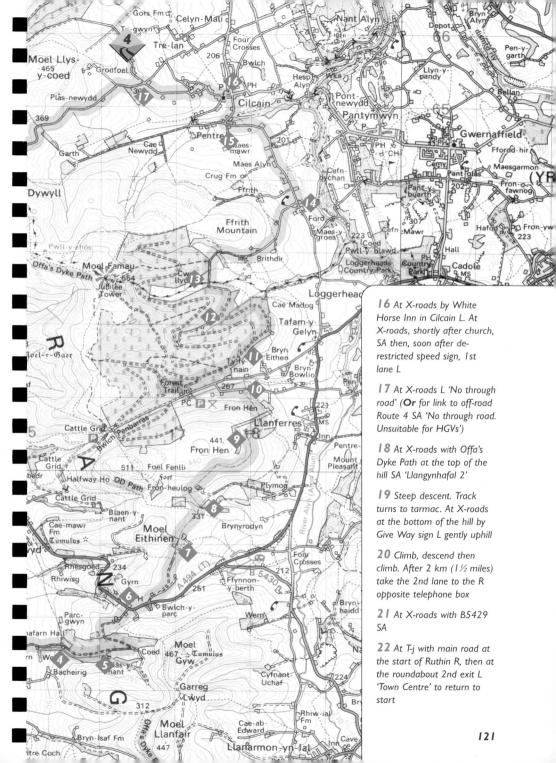

16 At X-roads by White Horse Inn in Cilcain L. At X-roads, shortly after church, SA then, soon after de-restricted speed sign, 1st lane L

17 At X-roads L 'No through road' (**Or** for link to off-road Route 4 SA 'No through road. Unsuitable for HGVs')

18 At X-roads with Offa's Dyke Path at the top of the hill SA 'Llangynhafal 2'

19 Steep descent. Track turns to tarmac. At X-roads at the bottom of the hill by Give Way sign L gently uphill

20 Climb, descend then climb. After 2 km (1½ miles) take the 2nd lane to the R opposite telephone box

21 At X-roads with B5429 SA

22 At T-j with main road at the start of Ruthin R, then at the roundabout 2nd exit L 'Town Centre' to return to start

6. Into the Berwyn Mountains, west of Oswestry

This his area of the country is poorly endowed with legal, rideable tracks and so the ride makes use of many of the unclassified roads, known variously as: UCRs; green lanes; white roads; county roads; class 4 and 5 roads or carriage roads. The Ordnance Survey Landranger sheet 124 covering Dolgellau is the first map in the series to show the existence of these rights of way, some of which provide the very best off-road cycling. This ride starts from Rhydycroesau to the west of Oswestry, passes through woodland close to the firing range (if firing is in progress, use the alternative route). After crossing the stream of Cynllaith the route climbs on-road then steeply off-road on a broad, stone track with marvellous views across the Ogau Valley. A long, grassy descent drops you down into valley with the inevitable climb out again, once more on a well-defined track. The track turns to grass and there is a muddy stretch through the forestry plantation before an undulating section and the final descent on tarmac back to the start.

Start
The village hall in Llawnt on the B4580 to the west of Oswestry

P As above

Distance
20 km (12 miles)

Strenuous

Terrain
Broadleaf woodland, sheep pasture and moorland. Total height gain – 505 m (1660 ft)

Nearest railway
Gobowen, 8 km (5 miles) northeast of Rhydycroesau

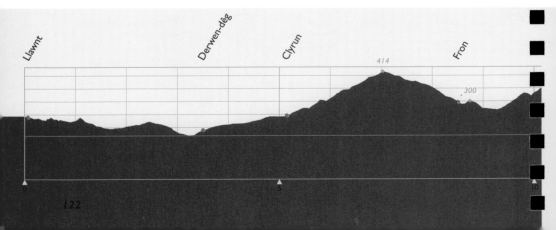

Llansilin near 4

Neat cottages line a narrow street that runs gently down past the old church to the greystone Wynnstay Arms, named after the Williams Wynn family whose estates in this part of the country were so great that the heads of

▼ Steep hill track to the west of Llangadwaladr

the family were dubbed the 'Princes in Wales'. The road running down the valley from Llansilin passes a prominent grassy mound – all that remains of Sycharth, home of Owain Glyndwr, the medieval Welsh patriot and hero

Old Oswestry Fort
east of the start
A hill-fort from about 250 BC with ramparts and ditches covering 22 ha (56 acres). The main entrance is flanked by pits, probably for water storage

Oswestry Bicycle Museum
east of the start
Over 100 bicycles illustrate the history and development of the bicycle. There are displays of early lighting from candle oil and carbon to battery and dynamo

Plenty of choice in **Oswestry** *(east of the start)* *Wynnstay Arms,* **Llansilin** *(off the route at instruction 4)* *West Arms PH* 🍴*, Hand PH* 🍴*,* **Llanarmon Dyffryn Ceiriog** *(off the route, to the west of instruction 10)*

Pensarn

432   419   433

325   379   344

169

1 At the X-roads on the B4580 near Llawnt Village Hall, take the minor road to the south 'Croesau Bach', then after 90 m (100 yd) turn R 'Pen-y-Dyffryn Hall Country Hotel'

2 Tarmac turns to narrow track. This is occasionally shut if firing is taking place. (See alternative route opposite)

3 Follow for 2 km (1½ miles) along the edge of the woodland. **Easy to miss.** 270 m (300 yd) after the narrow track turns to broad stone track by house 1st R downhill sharply back on yourself

4 Through ford or over bridge. Climb past house. At offset X-roads with B4580 R, then L 'Rhiwlas, Llangadwaladr, Llanarmon'

5 At T-j bear R (in effect SA) 'Rhiwlas, Llanarmon', then after 800 m (½ mile), shortly after the brow of the hill and the long stone buildings of Clyrun to the right, take the next track to the L 'Gyrn'

6 Rough, steep section immediately after the house. Long steady climb. Climb to high point where the track joins from the left

7 Track becomes grassy and continues gently downhill in the same direction alongside fence. Track improves. At fork bear R downhill. Through the farm at Fron

8 At offset X-roads of lanes R for 18 m (20 yd) 'Rhydleos', then 1st track L

9 After 1 km at fork after gate take the lower RH track to the R of the stream

10 At X-roads of tracks at the corner of coniferous woodland R

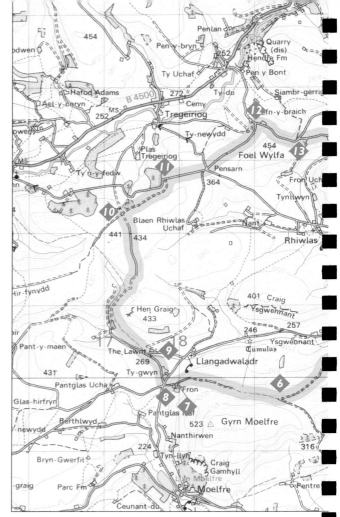

11 At T-j with road R. After 800 m (½ mile) 1st L 'Tregeiriog', then immediately R uphill on tarmac lane

12 At T-j by triangle of grass R towards and through farm

13 Climb for 400 m (¼ mile), at fork of tracks R

14 Track turns to grass. At X-roads with footpath sign to the right and bridleway sign to the left go SA

15 Enter forestry. Muddy section. At fork of tracks L, then At T-j L, go through gate and follow track (may be muddy) along edge of woodland

16 At rough junction of grassy tracks by two gates take the LH track between stone gateposts

17 The track turns to tarmac. At X-roads R to return to the start

Alternative route

Out of Rhydycroesau village hall car park and SA onto lane opposite 'Croesau Bach'. At X-roads after 3 km (2 miles) R 'Llnasilin'. Go past farm buildings and take first road R by triangle of grass. On sharp LH bend turn R onto track and rejoin route

Along the Mawddach Estuary, west of Dolgellau

Divided into three parts, this superb ride can be enjoyed by every sort of cyclist from a young child to a super-fit athlete. The first section runs west from Dolgellau along the course of the dismantled railway line by the Mawddach Estuary. There are beautiful views out across the sand banks to the crags and hills to the north. For those looking for an easy, flat outing the ride can be as short or as long as you want up to a maximum of 24 km (15 miles) if you go right to the end of the railway path and back again. Making the ride into a loop involves a very steep push on-road for over a kilometre. After climbing over 244 m (800 ft) almost all of the rest of the route is downhill back to Dolgellau, on a quiet lane beneath Cadair Idris. The full route includes a second loop that continues on to the small coastal village of Llwyngwril where there is the second (and last) chance of refreshments along the route. A second, steep on-road climb is followed at first on a rough track then on the remnants of the old mountain road up from Llanegryn. The second loop rejoins the first to pass beneath Cadair Idris back to Dolgellau.

Start

The Tourist Information, Eldon Square, Dolgellau

P Follow signs for long stay car park near river

Distance and grade

43 km (27 miles) — two loops of 24½+ 18½ km (15+11 miles). 24 km (15 miles) with short cut. Up to 24 km (15 miles) there and back on the railway path

🪃🪃🪃🪃🪃 Strenuous

🪃🪃🪃 Moderate with short cut

🪃 Easy there and back on the railway path

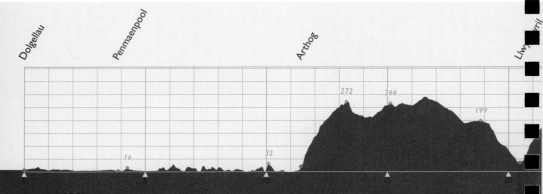

Terrain

Railway path alongside estuary, steep lanes, mountain tracks. Total height gain – 730 m (2395 ft) or 250 m (820 ft) on the moderate route. (The easy route has no hills!)

Nearest Railway

Llwyngwril, on the coast south of Barmouth

Places of interest

Dolgellau 1
Set on the banks of the River Wnion, the town's restrained, robust buildings are almost entirely made of the same dark boulder stone and lighter granite, which, from a distance, give the impression that the whole town has been carved from a single block of material. Livestock markets have been held here for centuries and in its time Dolgellau has been a centre for the wool trade, tanning, knitting and even gold prospecting

Torrent Walk *east of Dolgellau 1*
A spectacular riverside walk leads for over 1 km past waterfalls along the steep wooded banks of the Clywedog River

Cymer Abbey 1
Arched windows and intricately carved columns are among the ruins of the 12th-century Cistercian abbey on the river bank where the Mawddach and Wnion meet

▲ *The mighty peak of Cadair Idris looms almost 914 m (3000 ft) above the town of Dolgellau*

Refreshments

Plenty of choice in **Dolgellau**
King George III PH 🍺, **Penmaenpool**
Garthangarad PH, **Llwyngwril**

Pant-gwyn   Rhydcriw   Ffordd Ddu   Rhydwen

405   406

296   239   177

189

25   30   35   40   42.7

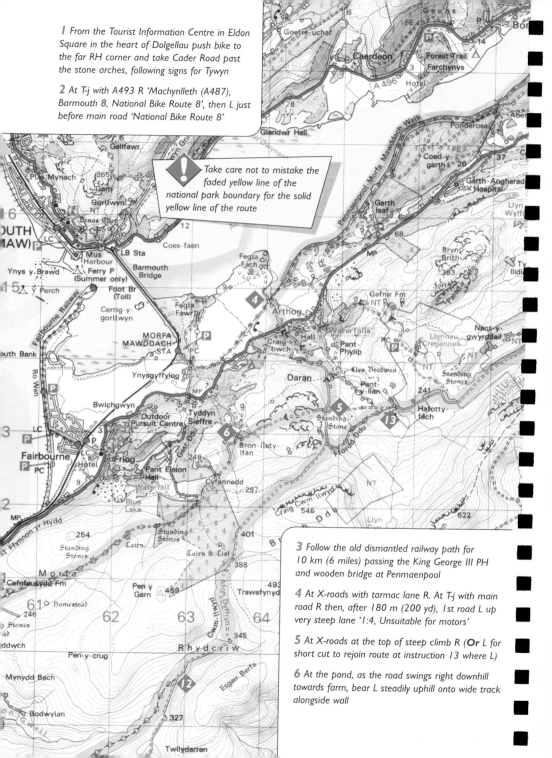

1 From the Tourist Information Centre in Eldon Square in the heart of Dolgellau push bike to the far RH corner and take Cader Road past the stone arches, following signs for Tywyn

2 At T-j with A493 R 'Machynlleth (A487), Barmouth 8, National Bike Route 8', then L just before main road 'National Bike Route 8'

Take care not to mistake the faded yellow line of the national park boundary for the solid yellow line of the route

3 Follow the old dismantled railway path for 10 km (6 miles) passing the King George III PH and wooden bridge at Penmaenpool

4 At X-roads with tarmac lane R. At T-j with main road R then, after 180 m (200 yd), 1st road L up very steep lane '1:4, Unsuitable for motors'

5 At X-roads at the top of steep climb R (**Or** L for short cut to rejoin route at instruction 13 where L)

6 At the pond, as the road swings right downhill towards farm, bear L steadily uphill onto wide track alongside wall

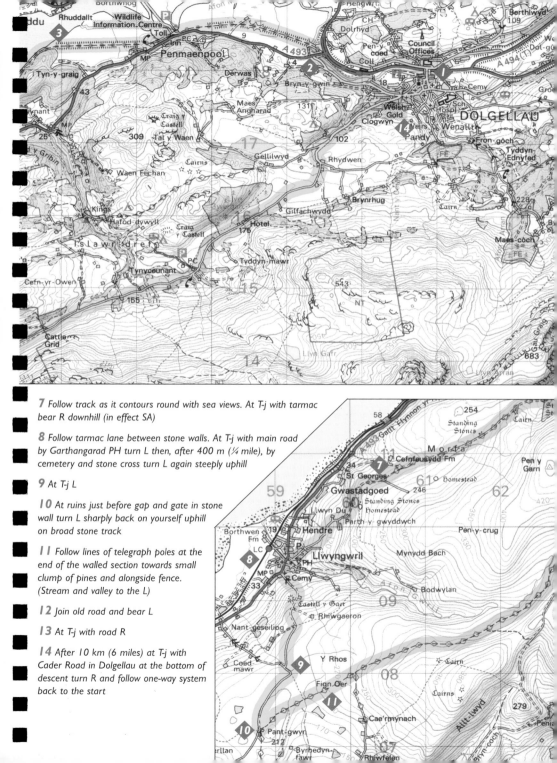

7 Follow track as it contours round with sea views. At T-j with tarmac bear R downhill (in effect SA)

8 Follow tarmac lane between stone walls. At T-j with main road by Garthangarad PH turn L then, after 400 m (¼ mile), by cemetery and stone cross turn L again steeply uphill

9 At T-j L

10 At ruins just before gap and gate in stone wall turn L sharply back on yourself uphill on broad stone track

11 Follow lines of telegraph poles at the end of the walled section towards small clump of pines and alongside fence. (Stream and valley to the L)

12 Join old road and bear L

13 At T-j with road R

14 After 10 km (6 miles) at T-j with Cader Road in Dolgellau at the bottom of descent turn R and follow one-way system back to the start

8 The Dovey Estuary and Happy Valley, west of Machynlleth

Start

The small car park on the A493 at Cwrt, 10 km (6 miles) to the west of Machynlleth

P As above

Distance and grade

25 km (15 miles)

Strenuous

Terrain

Mountain tracks and river valleys. Total height gain – 570 m (1870 ft)

Nearest railway

Machynlleth, 7 km (4 miles) east of the start

Two steep climbs out of Happy Valley, each rewarded with fantastic views, form the basis of this energetic ride to the west of Machynlleth. The first and steeper of the two climbs begins right at the start of the ride from Cwrt, first on tarmac, then on a broad stone track where you will probably have to get off and push. The high point is reached over 2 km (1½ miles) from the road and beyond here there is a long descent on an ever improving track. The miniature railway line of the Talyllyn Railway is crossed twice on the road section near to Tywyn, which offers the only refreshments close to the route. Happy Valley is joined and followed for 5 km (3 miles) before taking a track to cross the stream and climb steeply through woodland up onto the hillside lying between the Dovey Estuary and Happy Valley. A minor road is briefly joined and you have the option of dropping down to an excellent pub in Aberdovey (this will involve an extra 244 m (800 ft) of climbing to regain the route!) before the last off-road section through numerous gates back to the start in Cwrt.

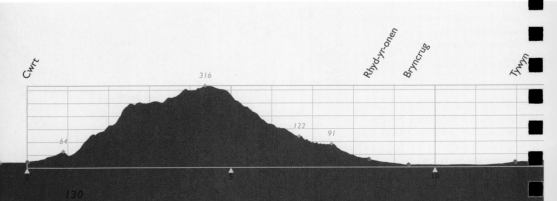

Refreshments

Plenty of choice in **Machynlleth** (east of the route)
Plenty of choice in **Tywyn**
Penhelig Arms PH ●●, **Aberdyfi** (3 km (2 miles) southwest of the route at instruction 10)

Places of interest

Centre for Alternative Technology
east of the start 1
A disused slate quarry houses a display explaining how energy can be supplied by sun, wind and water

Aberdovey 3 km (2 miles) southwest of the route at 10
An attractive seaside resort at the mouth of the River Dovey with a wide beach and the Maritime Museum in an old warehouse on the jetty. Quiet streets and squares of houses, built for sea captains lie behind the busy seafront

▼ Dovey Estuary, Ynys Las Nature Reserve

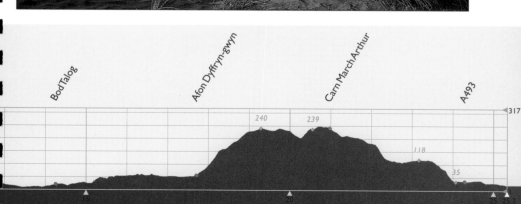

Take care not to mistake the faded yellow line of the national park boundary for the solid yellow line of the route

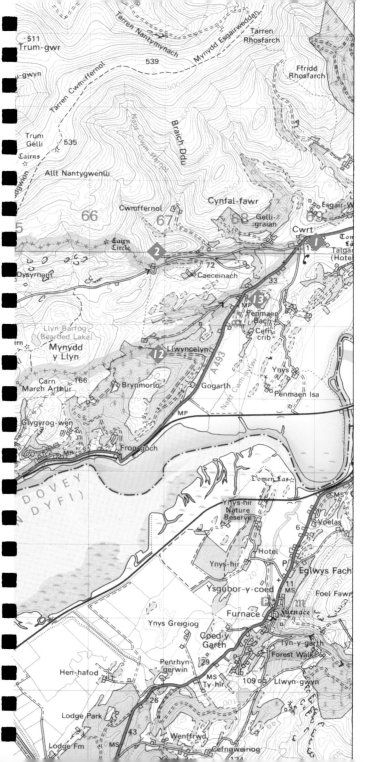

1 *Out of car park at Cwrt, cross road, then turn sharply L uphill '17 ton weight limit'*

2 *Climb steadily. After 1 km, at white house on LH bend, bear R onto wide stone track and climb steeply uphill through gate*

3 *At fork of tracks, shortly after reaching the top, bear R through gate (the LH fork is signed 'No horses')*

4 *The track turns to tarmac. Go over miniature railway and past caravan park. At T-j with more major road bear L. At T-j (with A493) L 'Tywyn 2'*

5 *After 2 km (1¼ miles) 1st lane to the L by sign for Tywyn at the start of the village 'National Cycle Network 8'*

6 *At T-j (with A493) L 'National Cycle Network 8', then 1st road L 'Cwm Maethlon, Happy Valley'*

7 **Easy to miss.** *After 5 km (3 miles), and 800 m (½ mile) after passing chapel and phone box on the left take the next R by wooden bungalow*

8 *Cross ford and bear R steeply uphill through wood*

9 *Exit wood and follow broad track sharply L uphill*

10 *At T-j with road at the top of steep climb L*

11 *Through gate, past house and onto track*

12 *Short muddy section. Rejoin tarmac by house*

13 *At T-j (with A493) L to return to the start*

Vyrnwy Valley and Dyfnant Forest north of Llangadfan

Start

Parking area at the junction of the B4395 with the A458, halfway between Dolgellau and Welshpool

🅿 As above

Distance and grade

34 km (21 miles)

///// Strenuous

Terrain

Farmland, river valleys and forestry. Total height gain – 585 m (1920 ft)

Nearest railway

Welshpool, 16 km (10 miles) east of the route at Dolanog

A tiny, quiet lane takes you from the small village of Llangadfan northeast up onto the ridge between the valleys of the Banwy and Vyrnwy Rivers, with wonderful views of both. This track, with its origins in the distant past, leads down into Dolanog. The river is followed to the northeast before striking north along one of its tributaries on a well-defined track through broadleaf woodland and sheep pastures. After a couple of kilometres on-road the route returns to bridleways and heads into one of the several blocks of forestry that make up Dyfnant Forest. As with all routes that use Forestry Commission tracks it is recommended that you take a compass with you and use it occasionally to check that you are heading in the right direction: new tracks are built, tree harvesting takes place and instructions may not appear to tally with what you see on the ground. In the case of Dyfnant Forest, set on the high ground between two river valleys, any track leading downhill will eventually lead into the network of lanes in one of them, from which it should be easy to work out a route back to Llangadfan.

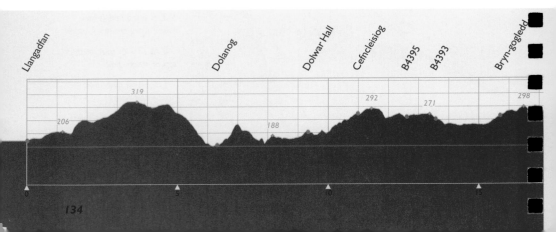

Dolanog 4

This small village nestling between the hill called Allt Dolanog and the River Vyrnwy is renowned for its association with the Welsh hymn writer Ann Griffiths, who died young and is buried with her two-week-old baby at nearby Llanfihangel. The name Dolanog comes from two Welsh words dol and eog which mean 'the dale of the salmon' and every autumn there is a wonderful display of salmon trying unsuccessfully to leap the waterfall on the Vyrnwy

Lake Vyrnwy *3 km (2 miles) northwest of the route at 14*

A reservoir created in 1881 and a superb example of Victorian ingenuity, built to supply water to Liverpool. 8 km (5 miles) long and 800 m (½ mile) wide, the lake is encircled by high peaks and tall pines. The mock-Gothic tower at the water's edge conceals the start of a 121 km (75 mile) pipeline. The visitor centre is in a converted chapel

▼ *Lake Vyrnwy Dam*

 Refreshments

Cann Office Inn, **Llangadfan**

Ddol Cownwy

Pren Croes

409

358

329

410

264

205

20

25

30

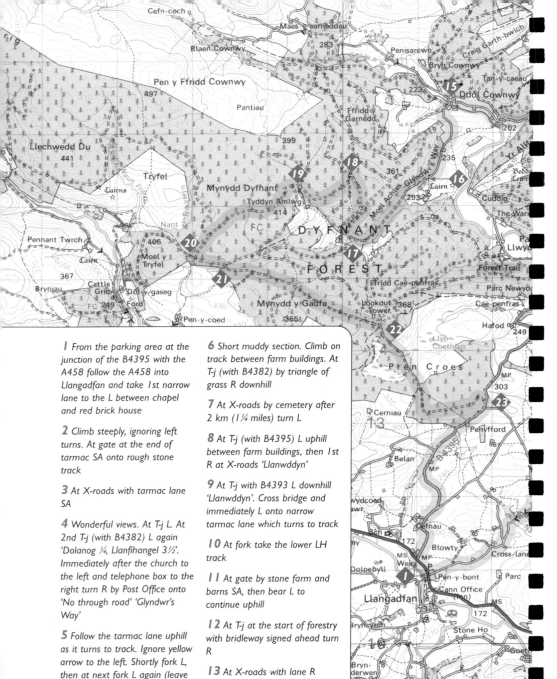

1 From the parking area at the junction of the B4395 with the A458 follow the A458 into Llangadfan and take 1st narrow lane to the L between chapel and red brick house

2 Climb steeply, ignoring left turns. At gate at the end of tarmac SA onto rough stone track

3 At X-roads with tarmac lane SA

4 Wonderful views. At T-j L. At 2nd T-j (with B4382) L again 'Dolanog ¼, Llanfihangel 3½'. Immediately after the church to the left and telephone box to the right turn R by Post Office onto 'No through road' 'Glyndwr's Way'

5 Follow the tarmac lane uphill as it turns to track. Ignore yellow arrow to the left. Shortly fork L, then at next fork L again (leave the Ann Griffith's Walk at this point)

6 Short muddy section. Climb on track between farm buildings. At T-j (with B4382) by triangle of grass R downhill

7 At X-roads by cemetery after 2 km (1¼ miles) turn L

8 At T-j (with B4395) L uphill between farm buildings, then 1st R at X-roads 'Llanwddyn'

9 At T-j with B4393 L downhill 'Llanwddyn'. Cross bridge and immediately L onto narrow tarmac lane which turns to track

10 At fork take the lower LH track

11 At gate by stone farm and barns SA, then bear L to continue uphill

12 At T-j at the start of forestry with bridleway signed ahead turn R

13 At X-roads with lane R downhill (**Or** L uphill for short cut back to the start)

14 At T-j with lane turn L sharply back on yourself downhill

15 Continue downhill through 'No through road' sign. Immediately after telephone box and 2nd 'No through road' sign bear L

16 At fork by sign for Maesdyfnant bear R on upper track

17 At fork by barrier and green posts (one post marked '50') bear

L on path over stream, then shortly next R

18 Ignore right turn. Continue uphill with stream to the left. At the next junction of tracks (GR 002164) opposite 'R30/17' signpost turn sharp L to continue climbing

19 At X-roads of tracks by 'R37' signpost go SA. Shortly, ignore left turn to continue SA

20 After I km ignore right signed 'R27' (GR 982155). Shortly, at T-j by '23' post, turn L

21 Short downhill section then, at fork by '22' post (GR 984151), bear R on lower track

22 Ignore several left turns at the top of the dip (posts 21 and 25)

23 Rejoin the road and turn R to return to the start

10 The Wye Valley and Hafren Forest, west of Llangurig

Start

The church in Llangurig, at the junction of the A470 and A44 north of Rhayader

P Car park in Llangurig on lane near Post Office heading south from the A44

Distance and grade

35 km (22 miles)

///// Strenuous

The sources of the River Wye and River Severn lie only 5 km (3 miles) apart on the eastern slopes of Plynlimon. This ride links the two rivers in their early, parallel stages. Although the first 8 km (5 miles) of this route are on-road, only the first kilometre is likely to carry traffic: after that you are on a no through road for 7 km (4 miles), climbing over 244 m (800 ft). The road drops down to a river where you are likely to get your feet wet as you ford its main tributary. Carry a compass through the woodland sections, regularly check progress against the map and accept that new tracks and forestry operations can often throw a spanner in the works. From the ford you have to climb then descend in a generally northward direction. The River Wye is followed northwest to within 5 km (3 miles) of its source. A magnificent, open descent briefly drops you down into the Severn Valley before the fourth and final, major climb of the day over the watershed. Once out of the forest a delightful riverside bridleway is followed for 3 km (2 miles) before the final on-road section back into Llangurig.

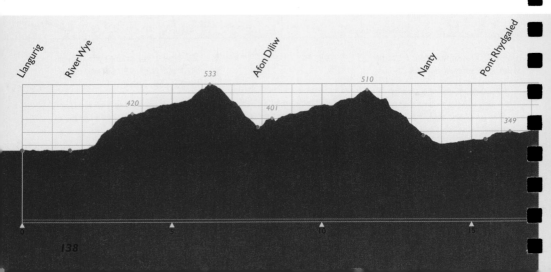

1 With back to the church in Llangurig L. After over 1 km, shortly after AA phone box and chevrons on RH bend, take the next road L 'Unsuitable for motors after 6 km (4 miles)'

2 Climb, then descend over 6 km (4 miles). Just before the river turn R through gate and follow track to cross the river just above the junction of two streams

3 Follow track steeply uphill with the major stream to the right. Go past exposed rock slabs to the left and towards ruined house on the horizon

4 Ignore right and left turns, go over the brow of hill, continuing SA at offset X-roads by a rocky outcrop to the left

5 Shortly, go SA at 2nd offset X-roads to emerge from forestry with field to the right

6 Soon after passing a sharp right turn down towards the farm take the next R downhill to the river (the main A44 is in sight and earshot)

7 At X-roads with a breeze block shed ahead turn R onto tarmac track and cross bridge. At T-j with A44 L, then R through farm 'Private Road'

8 Cross bridge over river (GR 831837) and continue SA with river now to your L

9 Pass barns and continue steadily uphill ignoring left turns

10 Climb past mining ruins. Descend into forest on fast track waymarked with purple and orange bike signs

11 Cross the stream (which passes through tunnel beneath forest road), then climb near to field. At T-j L (purple and orange markers) then 1st R steeply uphill

12 At T-j bear L uphill and L at fork with stream valley to the L

13 Keep bearing L, continuing to climb. Ignore left turn, then go SA through two X-roads (the 2nd is at the brow of the hill)

14 Descend, then gentle climb. Track joins from the right. With views opening up on the right turn R downhill and follow the track round to the L. After 800 m (½ mile) bear R downhill (keeping close to the river on the right) 'R501'

15 Exit forest via gate near to the river and enter field. The 1st 90 m (100 yd) are indistinct but the track becomes more defined

16 At X-roads with lane SA

17 At fork by ruin bear R uphill. Go past the ruin then continue in the same direction along an avenue of trees. At T-j with track R, then at road R again

18 At T-j with main road (A44) L to return to the start

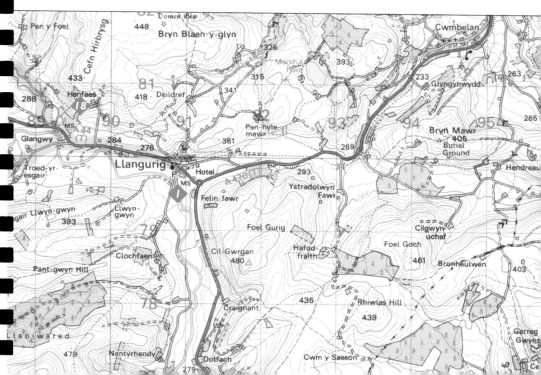

Cycle TOURS Cycle TOURS Cycle TOURS

The Ordnance Survey Cycle Tours series

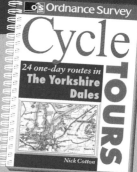

◆ **Around Birmingham**
◆ **Around London**
◆ **Avon, Somerset & Wiltshire**
◆ **Berks, Bucks & Oxfordshire**
◆ **Central Scotland**
◆ **Cornwall & Devon**
◆ **Cumbria & the Lakes**
◆ **Dorset, Hampshire & Isle of Wight**
◆ **East Anglia – South**
◆ **Gloucestershire and Hereford & Worcester**
◆ **Kent, Surrey & Sussex**
◆ **North Wales and The Marches**
◆ **North Yorkshire & Teesside**
◆ **Northumberland and County Durham**
◆ **Peak District**
◆ **Southern Scotland**
◆ **South, West and Mid-Wales**
◆ **Yorkshire Dales**

The whole series is available from all good bookshops or by mail order direct from the publisher. Payment can be made by credit card or cheque/postal order in the following ways:

By phone Phone your order through on our special *Credit Card Hotline* on *01733 371999 (Fax: 01733 370585)*. Speak to our customer service team during office hours (9am to 5pm) or leave a message on the answer machine, quoting your full credit card number plus expiry date and your full name and address and reference.

By post Simply fill out the order form (you may photcopy it) and send it to: *Reed Books Direct, 43 Stapledon Road, Orton Southgate, Peterborough PE2 6TD.*

Ordnance Survey Cycle TOURS ORDER FORM

I wish to order the following titles

Title	Quantity @ £9.99 each	£ Total
AROUND BIRMINGHAM	☐ 0 600 58623 5 ➤	☐
AROUND LONDON	☐ 0 600 58845 9 ➤	☐
AVON, SOMERSET & WILTSHIRE	☐ 0 600 58664 2 ➤	☐
BERKS, BUCKS & OXFORDSHIRE	☐ 0 600 58156 X ➤	☐
CENTRAL SCOTLAND	☐ 0 600 59005 4 ➤	☐
CORNWALL & DEVON	☐ 0 600 58124 1 ➤	☐
CUMBRIA & THE LAKES	☐ 0 600 58126 8 ➤	☐
DORSET, HAMPSHIRE & ISLE OF WIGHT	☐ 0 600 58667 7 ➤	☐
EAST ANGLIA – SOUTH	☐ 0 600 58125 X ➤	☐
GLOUCESTERSHIRE AND HEREFORD & WORCESTER	☐ 0 600 58665 0 ➤	☐
KENT, SURREY & SUSSEX	☐ 0 600 58666 9 ➤	☐
NORTH WALES AND THE MARCHES	☐ 0 600 59007 0 ➤	☐
NORTH YORKSHIRE & TEESSIDE (Available May '97)	☐ 0 600 59103 4 ➤	☐
NORTHUMBERLAND AND COUNTY DURHAM (Available May '97)	☐ 0 600 59105 0 ➤	☐
PEAK DISTRICT	☐ 0 600 58889 0 ➤	☐
SOUTHERN SCOTLAND	☐ 0 600 58624 3 ➤	☐
SOUTH, WEST AND MID-WALES	☐ 0 600 58846 7 ➤	☐
YORKSHIRE DALES	☐ 0 600 58847 5 ➤	☐

Name...

Address...

....

....Postcode

◆ **Free postage and packing**

◆ All available titles will normally be dispatched within 5 working days of receipt of order but please allow up to 28 days for delivery

◆ Whilst every effort is made to keep prices low, the publisher reserves the right to increase prices at short notice

☐ Please tick this box if you do not wish your name to be used by other carefully selected organisations that may wish to send you information about other products and services

Registered Office: Michelin House, 81 Fulham Road, London SW3 6RB. Registered in England number 1974080

I enclose a cheque/postal order, for a **total** of ☐

made payable to *Reed Book Services*, or please debit my

☐ Access   ☐ American Express   ☐ Visa   ☐ Diners

account by ☐

Account no

☐☐☐☐ ☐☐☐☐ ☐☐☐☐ ☐☐☐☐

Expiry date ☐☐ ☐☐

Signature...

Post to: Reed Books Direct, 43 Stapledon Road, Orton Southgate, Peterborough PE2 6TD